UNIVERSITY OF NORTH CAROLINA AT CHAPEL HILL
DEPARTMENT OF ROMANCE LANGUAGES

NORTH CAROLINA STUDIES
IN THE ROMANCE LANGUAGES AND LITERATURES

Founder: URBAN TIGNER HOLMES
Editor: STIRLING HAIG

Distributed by:

UNIVERSITY OF NORTH CAROLINA PRESS
CHAPEL HILL
North Carolina 27514
U.S.A.

NORTH CAROLINA STUDIES IN THE
ROMANCE LANGUAGES AND LITERATURES
Number 222

THE BROKEN ANGEL:
MYTH AND METHOD IN VALÉRY

The first quotation on page 95 should read as follows:

CORRECT TEXT

Mon cœur vous soit obscur!... Il me l'est à moi-même.
Tout démon que vous êtes, vous n'y pouvez rien comprendre. Après tout, vous n'êtes que le Diable. ... Il n'y a point
de musique en vous... Ô mon cœur, tu te moques du mal...
et même du bien... Mais vous, ... Tu n'es qu'esprit!... Mais
les Anges eux-mêmes, les Archanges bénêtes, tous ces fils de
lumière et ces puissances de ferveur ne peuvent pas comprendre... Ils sont purs, ils sont durs, ils sont forts. Mais
la tendresse!... Que voulez-vous que des êtres éternels puissent sentir le prix d'un regard, d'un instant, tout le don de
la faiblesse... le don d'un bien qu'il faut saisir entre le
naître et le mourir. Ils ne sont que lumière et tu n'es que
ténèbres... Mais moi, mais nous, nous portons nos clartés
et nous portons nos ombres... (O, II, 149)

THE BROKEN ANGEL:
MYTH AND METHOD IN VALÉRY

BY

URSULA FRANKLIN
GRAND VALLEY STATE COLLEGES

CHAPEL HILL

NORTH CAROLINA STUDIES IN THE ROMANCE
LANGUAGES AND LITERATURES
U.N.C. DEPARTMENT OF ROMANCE LANGUAGES

1984

Library of Congress Cataloging in Publication Data

Franklin, Ursula.
    The broken angel.

    (North Carolina studies in the Romance languages and literatures; no. 222.)
    Text in English and French.
    Bibliography: p.
    1. Valéry, Paul, 1871-1945—Criticism and interpretation.   2. Angels in literature.   3. Myth in literature.
    I. Title.   II. Series.
    PQ2643.A26Z612 1984   848'.91209   84-1590
    ISBN 0-8078-9226-2

I.S.B.N. 0-8078-9226-2

IMPRESO EN ESPAÑA

PRINTED IN SPAIN

DEPÓSITO LEGAL: V. 821 - 1984   I.S.B.N. 84-499-7086-5

ARTES GRÁFICAS SOLER, S. A. - LA OLIVERETA, 28 - VALENCIA (18) - 1984

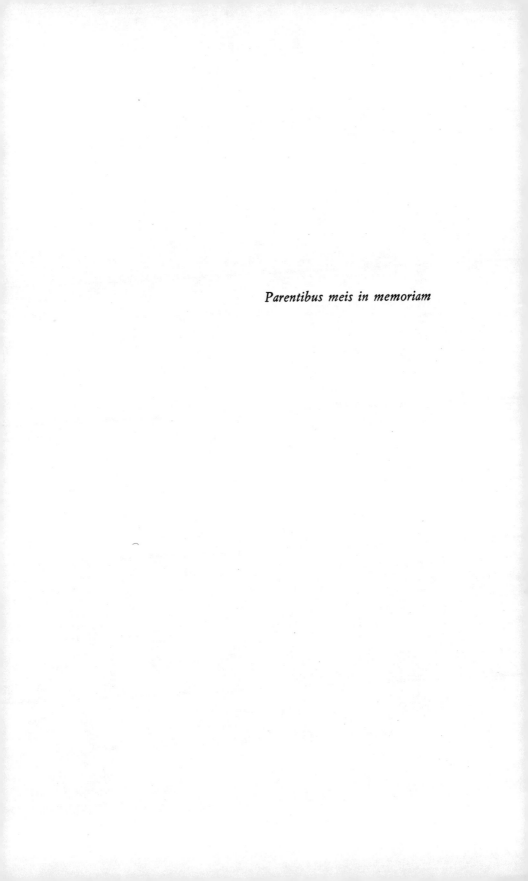

Parentibus meis in memoriam

FOREWORD

The Angel is a mythopoetic configuration that pervades Valéry's entire textual universe; linked to almost every one of its themes, the figure in-forms all of its modes — from personal letters and notes in the *Cahiers* to lyric, dramatic, and discursive expression — which, in turn, form and de-form it. This study is an attempt to delineate the traces of these transformations.

I am grateful for a Fellowship from the American Council of Learned Societies which enabled me to work in Paris. And I wish to express my special gratitude to Mme Nicole Celeyrette-Pietri for generous advice and encouragment, to Mme Florence de Lussy of the Bibliothèque Nationale and M. François Chapon of the Bibliothèque littéraire Jacques Doucet for granting me access to documents crucial to the preparation of this study.

I thank the editors of *The Centennial Review, The Romanic Review* and *Comparative Literature* for their kind permission to use material which first appeared in their journals. My thanks go to Professor Stirling Haig of the University of North Carolina Studies in the Romance Languages and Literatures for exceptional help with the manuscript. I have quoted extensively from the poetry and prose of Valéry by permission of the copyright holders, Editions Gallimard, Paris.

Finally, my deepest indebtedness is to my friend and teacher, Professor John A. Yunck, without whose untiring criticism and counsel this study could not have been completed.

U. F.

TABLE OF CONTENTS

INTRODUCTION

The voluminous and frequently controversial literature [1] on Valéry abounds in studies exploring individual poems and collections, the *Dialogues,* dramatic work and critical essays, as well as the *œuvre* as a whole. While the characteristics of their themes and imagery, Valéry's psychological complexities and his ideological orientation(s) have been subject to critical discourse for over fifty years, more recently commentators have concentrated on the stylistic and linguistic aspects of his work. The publication of the *Notebooks* [2] and some of the correspondence [3] has stimulated investigations of Valéry's sources and of the more delicate problem of influence; it has, moreover, yielded important studies of the evolution of motifs and themes in those *Notebooks* and from the *Cahiers* to the œuvre. [4] A few years ago we demonstrated the significance of Valéry's contribution to the prose poem, [5] that rather vaguely defined *genre* whose transformation in Valéry pointed to the emergence of the "mobile

---

[1] Cf. Philippe Sollers in *Le Monde,* 29 October 1971, where he calls Valéry "le représentant d'une culture finissante" and attacks the poet severely for "not understanding anything of the literature of his time."

[2] Paul Valéry, *Cahiers,* 29 volumes (ed. facsimile, Paris: C.N.R.S., 1957-61). All quotations from Valéry's *Cahiers* will refer to this edition, unless otherwise indicated, and be identified by the word "Cahiers," volume and page number.

[3] Paul Valéry, *Lettres à quelques-uns* (Paris: Gallimard, 1952); *André Gide-Paul Valéry, Correspondance 1887-1942* (Paris: Gallimard, 1955); *Paul Valéry-Gustave Fourment, Correspondance 1887-1933* (Paris: Gallimard, 1957).

[4] Cf. Edmée de la Rochefoucauld, *En lisant les Cahiers de Paul Valéry,* 3 vols. (Paris: Editions Universitaires, 1967); Judith Robinson, *Analyse de l'esprit dans les Cahiers de Valéry* (Paris: Corti, 1963); and above all, Nicole Celeyrette-Pietri's magistral *Valéry et le Moi des Cahiers à l'œuvre* (Paris: Klincksieck, 1979).

[5] Ursula Franklin, *The Rhetoric of Valéry's Prose Aubades* (Toronto: University of Toronto Press, 1979).

fragment," a morphological outgrowth of the poet's creative technique. [6]

This study deals with one of Valéry's major mythopoetic configurations: the angel, a recurring symbolic image of his lyric poetry and an obsessive myth that pervades his entire poetic universe. In tracing the construction and destruction of the figure inherited from tradition, that is its *défiguration,* we will find it closely linked to the poet's method of composition, the construction and weaving of anterior segments into texts, many of which remain open-ended and fragmentary. At the same time, the broken form of Valéry's texts on the angel is conditioned by the very tensions inherent in the theme, tensions which we intend here to examine. The fragmented angel, moreover, has antecedents in the work of the young Valéry's Master, Mallarmé.

If God has indeed succumbed in the Schopenhauerian *Götterdämmerung* that has thrown its shadows over the last century and our own, the angels, paradoxically, have not: they subsist, numerous though secularized, in the most diverse sorts of poetic discourse from Romanticism to our day. In a recent study we demonstrated how Mallarmé's early angelology was influenced by Lamartine and especially Hugo, [7] before it became secularized, partly through the poet's encounter with the poetic angels of Poe. Likewise significant is the great angelic *Prelude* to *Der Teppich des Lebens* of Mallarmé's German Symbolist disciple, Stefan George, while the predominant role of the angel in the work of the other great twentieth-century German poet, Rainer Maria Rilke, is a critical commonplace. The latter's angelology culminates in his late work, the *Duineser Elegien* which, as he frequently stated, could not have been completed without the inspiring encounter with the poetry of Valéry. [8] Symbolist poetry, that at times wishes to supplant a dead religion, is at its heart a paradoxical expression of absence and of presence, of renun-

---

[6] Cf. my "Toward the Prose Fragment in Mallarmé and Valéry: *Igitur* and *Agathe*," *French Review,* 49, 4, 536-48; "Structural Variations on a Theme: The Mobile Fragments of Valéry's Prose Aubades," *Michigan Academician,* X, 2, 163-79.

[7] "Segregation and Disintegration of an Image: Mallarmé's Struggle with the Angel," to appear in *Nineteenth-Century French Studies.*

[8] Cf. Monique St. Hélier, *A Rilke pour Noël* (Bern: Editions du Chandelier, 1927), p. 21.

ciation and acceptance: and the expression of this tension between polar opposites centers for Mallarmé and for Valéry, as it frequently does for their German disciples, on the same symbolic figure: the angel, vestige of a former age.

In our recent examination of the Mallarméan angel, we traced the poet's early segregation of the image from its childhood associations, and then followed its subsequent explosive fragmentation, with the residual fragments assuming a progressively richer symbolic significance. In Mallarmé's later poetry the angel as such had — like the universal order of which he was once a part — become meaningless while his transmuted fragments expanded into new nuclei of meaning. At the same time Mallarmé's language was suffering a similar fragmentation, or syntactic dislocation, reflecting a new poetic cosmos. Does Mallarmé's poetry, we asked, also reflect, indirectly, the "Copernican Revolution" of a contemporary philosopher whom he had probably never read? Schopenhauer, who influenced Valéry's early angels, had inverted the old *Weltanschauung,* according to which our world, though often apparently meaningless in its parts, was reasonable in its entirety. For the great anti-Hegelian, on the contrary, the universe, though logical in its fragments, is, considered in its entirety, without sense or reason, logic and reason being themselves the passing byproducts merely of its blind forces. Both Mallarmé and the philosopher agreed, moreover, that art can give man respite from those blind forces that will ultimately destroy him, as they have formed him, by chance.

Valéry, soon emancipated from both the Mallarméan influence and the Schopenhauerian ambiance that prevailed during the Symbolist period, came to form his idols precisely of that reason and logic which they had rejected, an "esprit" conveyed through the image of the Angel. In this study we intend to trace the construction of that myth and to show how closely it is associated with the creative method that both formed and deformed it. Finally, our reading must — *pace* Formalists! — take account of the evident: the existential situation and psychological predispositions of an *Ego scriptor* whose Broken Angel emerges from broken texts.

CHAPTER I

BEGINNINGS UNDER THE SIGN OF MALLARMÉ
AND SCHOPENHAUER

Valéry repeatedly and eloquently expressed his love and vene-
ration for the poet who changed his art, whose influence haunted
his life, in the Mallarmé essays of the twenties and thirties, the
"letter" concerning the "Coup de dés," the beautiful prose poem
celebrating his "Dernière Visite à Mallarmé," and finally in an essay
published in 1944, the year before his death.[1] In the "Lettre sur
Mallarmé," which appeared in 1927 in *La Revue de Paris*, Valéry,
by then France's most celebrated poet, reminisces:

> A l'âge encore assez tendre de vingt ans, et au point
> critique d'une étrange et profonde transformation intellec-
> tuelle, je subis le choc de l'œuvre de Mallarmé: je connus
> la surprise, le scandale intime instantané, et l'éblouissement,
> et la rupture de mes attaches avec mes idoles de cet âge. Je
> me sentis devenir comme fanatique; j'éprouvai la progres-
> sion foudroyante d'une conquête spirituelle décisive. (*O*, I,
> 637)

Henri Mondor retraced the first steps of that friendship, from the
letters written to the Master by the young poet, "un jeune homme
perdu au fond de la province," to their first meeting at the rue de
Rome apartment in October of 1891.[2] In the first letter of October

---

[1] Paul Valéry, *Œuvres* I (Paris: Gallimard, 1957; II, 1960), 619-710. All
quotations from Valéry's work will refer to this edition, unless otherwise
indicated, and be identified with the letter *O*, volume and page number.

[2] Henri Mondor, *L'Heureuse Rencontre de Valéry et de Mallarmé* (Lausanne: La Guilde du Livre, 1947).

1890, the nineteen-year-old law student at Montpellier professes himself "profondément pénétré des doctrines savantes du grand Edgar Allan Poe — peut-être le plus subtil artiste de ce siècle." In the second, of April 1891, he again declares his devotion to Poe and thus, by extension, to Mallarmé: "une dévotion toute particulière à Edgar Poe me conduit alors à donner pour royaume au poète, l'analogie. Il précise l'écho mystérieux des choses, et leur secrète harmonie, aussi réelle, aussi certaine qu'un rapport mathématique à tous esprits artistes, c'est-à-dire, et comme il sied, idéalistes violents..." [3] From the beginning then, Valéry assumes the credo of the Master in the cult of his hero, just as the worship of Richard Wagner had passed down from Baudelaire to Mallarmé and his heirs. To identify himself as disciple, the young poet professes the Master's religion.

We use this term advisedly, for when Valéry years later recalls that movement, loosely termed "Symbolism," he tells us that it was indeed a sort of religion: "... cette dévotion à l'art pur dont je vous parlais? Le simple exposé de cet état m'oblige à employer pour le décrire des termes qui ne se trouvent que dans le vocabulaire le plus religieux" ("Existence du Symbolisme," O, I, 698). We must understand this ambiance, for out of it grew Valéry's early poetry, such as the sonnet "Le Jeune Prêtre" and "La Suave Agonie," poems which he enclosed in his first letters to Mallarmé (O, I, 1578 and 1581-82), as well as the "Narcisse parle" mentioned in the second one (O, I, 1551 ff.) and on which Mallarmé comments in his reply.

Valéry's first two letters to Mallarmé and the three poems, these earliest of his metapoetic and poetic texts, contain in ovo the destiny of the poet and one of his major myths, the Angel. When the nineteen-year-old poet tells Mallarmé that the fragments of his poetry, discovered in various journals by chance, instilled in him the desire "[de] se joindre, avec son rêve personnel, aux quelques amants de la chasteté esthétique," he already stresses his own autonomy — "son rêve personnel" — the religious character of a select order, and an aesthetic theory guided by Poe, some of whose principles he then enumerates: "les poèmes courts, concentrés pour un éclat final, où les rythmes sont comme les marches marmoréennes de l'autel que couronne le dernier vers!" Some of the tenets of "The Philosophy

---

[3] Valéry, *Lettres à quelques-uns,* pp. 28, 47.

of Composition" and "The Poetic Principle" are clothed here in the religious imagery which characterizes the two enclosed poems that attempt to demonstrate the theory.

All his life Valéry remained faithful to this early allegiance to Poe the aesthetician and theoretician: and his angel is marked by that inspiration; by "Eureka" and "The Domain of Arnheim," rather than "Israfel." The early Valéryan angel, moreover, grew out of the vaguely religious and escapist atmosphere shared by Mallarmé's young admirers, friends like Pierre Louÿs, who introduced him and his poetry to the Master, and André Gide, the author of *Les Cahiers* and *Les Poésies d'André Walter,* fellow disciples of the rue de Rome, with whom near Narcissa's tomb in the Botanical Garden at Montpellier, Valéry dreamed about emulating Mallarméan perfection. [4]

The correspondence of Valéry and his new friend André Gide, which records the beginnings of a famous friendship and the early phases of two distinguished artistic careers, also reveals vividly the flavor of the "chapelle" and the language of the young apostles of Symbolism. These letters frequently constitute, moreover, essays at "écriture," containing passages which subsequently found their way into Valéry's prose poems. [5] In a letter of December 1890, Valéry "celebrates" the liturgy and ritual admired by the young poets and which inspired poems like "Le Jeune Prêtre":

> ...Demain, à la petite messe basse, j'irai surprendre les mys-
> térieux éclats de l'or ciborial sous le cierge, comme le prêtre
> ira de fidèle à fidèle portant l'hostie au bout des doigts!
> Et j'irai aussi à la grande! Quand, dans la bouche de l'évê-
> que mitré et splendide, le latin des proses évangéliaires

---

[4] The Edinburgh Valéry Colloquium has brought to light new documentation on Valéry's early friendships, and especially on the complex question of Mallarmé's "influence" on the younger poet. The contributions by Barbier and Lawler (*Colloque Paul Valéry,* Paris: Nizet, 1978), pp. 49-83, "Valéry et Mallarmé jusqu'en 1898," Carl C. Barbier; pp. 85-103, "Valéry et Mallarmé: Le Tigre et la Gazelle," James R. Lawler) redefine this classic case of what Harold Bloom has termed "the anxiety of influence" (Harold Bloom, *The Anxiety of Influence: A Theory of Poetry,* [London: Oxford University Press, 1973]) in modern literature.

[5] Cf. my " 'Les Vieilles Ruelles,' 'Pages inédites,' and 'Purs Drames': A Dialectical Triad of Three Early Prose Poems by Paul Valéry" in *Kentucky Romance Quarterly* (Summer, 1979), 81-94.

ranimera les ferveurs pâlissantes et rallumera pour un instant
le magique Sirius des trois rois fabuleux. [6]

And in February 1891, responding to Gide's famous announcement
of his own place in the new school ("donc Mallarmé pour la poésie,
Maeterlinck pour le drame — et..., j'ajoute Moi pour le roman"),
Valéry congratulates his friend in terms which, indeed, "ne se trouvent que dans le vocabulaire le plus religieux":

> Mon cher caloyer du mont symbolique,
> Deux mots à la hâte pour vous féliciter de cette conversion
> miraculeuse et divinement fatale; car tous les esprits brû-
> lants et purs viennent toujours enfin à l'adoration des très
> saintes Icônes de l'art, dans la chapelle ultime et délicieuse
> du Symbolisme. [7]

In this rarified atmosphere, and out of this ardent correspondence, rises the hieratic figure of Valéry's first angel. In a letter of
April 1891, commenting disdainfully on a review of his "Narcisse
parle" that had appeared in Le Journal des Débats, Valéry first makes
a profession of faith in Mallarmé's religion: "je suis de ceux pour
qui le livre est saint. On en fait UN, qui est le bon et le seul de
son être, et l'on disparaît." Then, after reminiscing on Baudelaire,
he paints a magnificent golden angel:

> ...Ma tristesse n'est pas de ce monde. Au seuil rude du sé-
> pulcre, surgit un ange d'or. Chu de l'azur facile aux portes
> de la tombe, il garde la pudeur de l'ombre merveilleuse.
> Et repose le funèbre trésor derrière ses ailes éblouies. Il
> protège le gracile sommeil des vierges de la Mort. Ses yeux
> sont clos, sa bouche close. Et moi, je veux lui faire dire
> le secret. Et je lui parle au crépuscule; au commencement
> pâle de la nuit heurtant d'une voix vaine le silence. Mais
> Lui, taciturne et splendide, soulève lentement, saintement
> ses paupières. Et me montre la flamme des yeux — de ses
> yeux qui ont vu le songe du Très Pur, qui ont vu jadis dans
> les lumières le songe peut-être du grand Dieu! [8]

---

[6] *Gide-Valéry Correspondance,* p. 41.
[7] Ibid., pp. 46, 48.
[8] Ibid., p. 80.

The angel with whom the poet converses on the threshold of the tomb, whose eyes are aflame from the vision of the "Très Pur," reappears two letters later in a passage, parts of which were to inspire the prose poem "Purs Drames," published the following year:

> Venez donc réveiller les antiques roses et les lis pen-
> chés comme un ange de jadis, un ange terrible et frêle de
> jadis dont un souffle aurait des corolles suscité l'éveil rose
> dans les jardins, et qui des gestes de ses mains aurait fait
> obéissants les parfums pâles et les feuilles confuses, dans
> l'Éden? [9]

In the Narcissistic angel, aglow with a vision of Purity, Gide recognizes his friend, whom he salutes, in a letter of June of that year: "vous êtes un ange de lumière, Paul-Ambroise..." [10] The recognition is both perceptive and highly significant: from the beginning, Valéry's Angel is linked to the Narcissus theme, as reflection and aspiration of the Self.

As it happens frequently in Mallarmé, and especially in "Les Fenêtres," the angel is associated in Valéry's early writing with the Fall; fallen from paradise unto "the gates of the tomb, he arises at the harsh threshold of the sepulchre," his golden radiance contrasting with night and death. The passage weaves contrapuntally the opposites of light and darkness, a celestial Eden and the here and now, timelessness and death. It celebrates chastity — "pudeur, vierges" — and purity: the eyes that have beheld them are flames in the night. And the "terrible and frail" angel of the other letter again evokes a memory of Eden.

Other poems of that period, some anterior to the letters, reflect the same motifs of isolation, chastity, and spiritual elevation clothed in the religious imagery traditionally associated with the angel. A poem significantly entitled "Solitude," dating from 1887, reads like a poetic reflection of Des Esseintes (the poet did not encounter Huysmans until 1889):

---

[9] Ibid., p. 83.
[10] Ibid., p. 99.

Loin du monde, je vis tout seul comme un hermite
Enfermé dans mon cœur mieux que dans un tombeau.
Je raffine mon goût du bizarre et du beau,
Dans la sérénité d'un rêve sans limite.

The sonnet's tercets stress again chastity and light, finally culminating in an elevation out of this world and beyond the angels themselves:

Je méprise les sens, les vices, et la femme,
Moi qui puis évoquer dans le fond de mon âme
La lumière... le son, la multiple beauté!

Moi qui puis combiner des voluptés étranges
Moi dont le rêve peut fuir dans l'immensité
Plus haut que les vautours, les astres et les anges...!

(*O*, I, 1585)

This isolation, chastity and scorn for woman prepares for the vocation of "Le Jeune Prêtre," the young man in black, protected from life's troubling temptations "sous les calmes cyprès d'un jardin clérical." In the sonnet's tercets, we see the young priest aspire to the angelic, thirsting to be raised to a sword-bearing archangel, in order to fight with the light against darkness:

Et — se dressent ses mains faites pour l'ostensoir,
Cherchant un glaive lourd! car il lui semble voir
Au couchant ruisseler le sang doré des anges!

Là-haut! il veut nageant dans le Ciel clair et vert
Parmi les Séraphins hardés de feux étranges,
Au son du cor, choquer du fer contre l'Enfer...!

(*O*, I, 1578)

In a sonnet of the following year, the poet again takes up the motifs of isolation, chastity and purity in celebrating the Immaculate Virgin, "Très loin du baiser fauve et flétrissant de l'homme!" She is "of marble, of metal cold and clear," and thus recalls another virgin, Mallarmé's Hérodiade. The artist will drink his inspiration from this pure chalice:

N'es-tu pas le Calice adorable de Chair
Où l'artiste — blanc prêtre de la magique phrase —
Boit à long traits le vin suprême de l'Extase?

(O, I, 1580)

Here priest and poet become one in the "artist — white priest of the magic phrase."

In a letter to Pierre Louÿs of October 1890, written a few days after the first letter to Mallarmé, Valéry announces that he is working on a poem, fragments of which have come down to us: "Je songe à une œuvre intitulée (Messe angélique), dont je vous livre en pâture la molle et détestable portion—hélas! figée. Combien lointaine du rêve échafaudé?" [11] This poem, as its title suggests, celebrates a liturgical angel:

O luminaires! ô vous, solitaires cierges,
Astres pudiques par les saintes mains des Vierges
Allumés comme les gardiens d'un pur trésor!
. . . .
Car l'Archange à l'autel de lune lentement
Pour la suave et blanche cérémonie
Apparaît (telle une lumière sur les eaux).
. . . .
Parmi les doux voiles d'argent des aromates
L'ange murmure des prières délicates
D'où naîtront pour la tristesse et les voluptés
Ces âmes par qui les hommes seront domptés.
. . . .
O luminaires! ô vous, solitaires flammes
Qu'entretiennent les mains saintes des saintes femmes,
Voici qu'il pleure l'ange aux cheveux éclatants.

(O, I, 1589-90)

One cannot regret that Valéry never finished the poem, whose conventionality borders on the banal. Yet this unoriginal celebration of the rite of the religion of art contains some important Valéryan motifs: luminosity, isolation, chastity, and purity.

But Valéry even at the age of nineteen is already sufficiently objective to explain that some of these elements, and especially the Schopenhauerian contempt for woman, were simply part of the poetic

---

[11] Valéry, *Lettres à quelques-uns,* p. 31.

and artistic ideology of the day; in a letter to a friend, the young
poet explains:

> ...Une très SYMPATHIQUE Ecole est venue trancher la
> difficulté d'une manière tout inattendue mais profondément
> ARTISTE...
> Ce siècle qui meurt, a de mille façons étudié, disséqué
> exalté ou honni cet Eternel Féminin... C'est alors qu'appa-
> raissent dans les ŒUVRES et dans les VIES, les plus éton-
> nantes fantaisies, les créations les plus bizarres. Edgar Poë
> enfante toute une galerie d'êtres féminins, ou plutôt aux
> apparences féminines, presque sans sexe, doués d'une vie
> surnaturelle, instruits des plus abstruses sciences, tels que
> sa Morella, familière avec la théologie et les beautés mathé-
> matiques.
> . . . .
> Enfin, prononçant le définitif anathème, vient Scho-
> penhauer qui condamne radicalement la femelle, et de qui
> procède toute cette jeune ECOLE dont je te parlais il y a
> quelques lignes.
> Pour elle, la femme n'existe plus. Toute la tendresse,
> tout l'épanchement qu'elle occasionnait jadis — on le re-
> porte vers de vagues formes CATHOLIQUES. On ne craint
> pas de parler à je ne sais quel Dieu avec l'équivoque parole
> et l'ardeur d'un amour de chair.
> . . . .
> Ce regain de ferveur religieuse, dont les Verlaine, les
> Huysmans (et quelques pages curieuses) voire les Mallarmé,
> sont les magnifiques Apôtres, n'a pas d'autres racines, que
> le dédain du Sexe bête.
> Quelle chose curieuse de voir produire en notre siècle,
> des œuvres d'une émotion mystique aussi intense que "Par-
> sival", que certaines pièces d'"AMOUR" [Verlaine] ou de
> L'ALBUM DE VERS ET DE PROSE. (Mallarmé). [12]

These conventions in which Valéry's early poetry participated, and
which the young poet, moreover, already understood with the objective clarity of a "regard d'ange," elucidate his poetic angels diachron-
ically, and indicate the relationship between the Angel and the
"Narcisse," enamored of his own solitary purity and beauty. But
underlying tensions — "la tristesse et les voluptés" — are already

---

[12] Bibliothèque Littéraire Jacques Doucet, Paul Valéry catalogue Pré-Teste,
n.° 113.

manifest in an angel's tears: "Voici qu'il pleure l'ange aux cheveux éclatants." For the Angel is not merely symptomatic of the Schopenhauerian artistic climate at the end of the nineteenth century, but also of a young man's struggles with the flesh, soon to produce a crisis which would profoundly transform both Narcissus and Angel.

Valéry frequently alludes to his "crise sentimentale aiguë" (O, I, 19-20) in his letters to Gide from 1891 to 1892. The young Montpellierian had fallen in love with a woman he had never met; and he now both suffers and analyzes the near fatal tortures that a mere mental image, her image in his mind, inflicts on him. He is both terrified and fascinated by the psychic process in which the mind is threatened with annihilation by its own creations and phantasms: "ce qu'il y a de plus illustre dans ces nouveautés, c'est que tout le Drame était mien (etait? est). Je me suis donné le spectacle de l'Amour.. Mais cette fois tout a hurlé. L'*esprit pur,* familier des *méditations,* s'est enfui tout mordu." [13] To his distant idol, Valéry writes love letters *expressing* what he suffers, which he does not send — "elle me laisse immobile avec mes lettres inutiles dans un tiroir" [14] — while to his friend he writes letters *analyzing* what is happening to him.

He writes, then, two series of letters, a written reflection of that *dédoublement intérieur* so characteristic of him, which underlies his life-long preoccupation with the myth of Narcissus. Valéry himself identifies his divided introspective self with the mythopoetic figure as he reports to Gide, in a letter of March 1892: "quant à Narcisse, il a écrit une lettre de plus à son tiroir et régularise une émotion par la bêtise." [15] One month later, he images this psychic schism by means of an internal drama of which he is both actor and beholder: "dans toute cette affaire, je mérite des sifflets et des pommes cuites, sauf au second acte où mon ange gardien m'a dicté de ces belles paroles lucides dont l'écriture soigneusement conservé me sera, demain, de l'intime gloire et une espèce d'encouragment futur à mieux gesticuler, et dire mon rôle." But the play is a dangerous one, for "j'ai failli me détruire deux ou trois fois: d'abord, de ne rien assouvir; ensuite et contradictoirement d'être aussi sot, identique

---

[13] *Gide-Valéry, Correspondance,* p. 110.
[14] Ibid., p. 122.
[15] Ibid., p. 130.

et tout humain; ce qui est le comble du mauvais goût. Constatation dont l'existence a racheté la mienne, m'ayant précipité dans l'analyse de ce en quoi je *devais* me différencier... des autres gens." [16]

The tone of youthful self-irony apart, this early letter already identifies three of Valéry's most characteristic traits: the consciousness of a dangerous vulnerability of the self; its mechanism of survival through self-analysis; and a rejection of the "human," of the *semblable,* in the self. All of these lead him to a dramatic resolution of his sentimental crisis later that year, culminating in the event commonly referred to as "la nuit de Gênes," a striking spiritual conversion not very dissimilar from those experienced and recorded by some of his great predecessors: the famous Night of Pascal, the Dream of Descartes, and finally, the "crise de Tournon" of the young Mallarmé.

Valéry emerges from the "nuit effroyable - passé sur mon lit - orage partout - ma chambre éblouissante par chaque éclair - Et tout mon sort se jouait dans ma tête. Je suis entre moi et moi" (*O, I,* 20). He is now victorious over the old self. A lucid *moi angélique,* the "esprit pur," has defeated the destructive passion and is now ready to renounce also a literary career, or for that matter any "career" other than the unique and solitary adventure of his mind. Retrospectively, the poet notes in one of his *Cahiers* in the twenties, under the heading "Mémoires de moi": "J'ai travaillé à ma façon à un travail sans nom et sans objet de 1892 à 1912..(et après, mais non plus exclusivement) sans encouragement aucun, sans *fin,* sans œuvre visée, - sans autre objet que de faire ma vision parfaitement accordée avec mes vraies questions, mes vraies forces" (*Cahiers,* XIII, 107). To harmonize one's vision perfectly with one's strength is the angelic, the super-human, aspiration.

---

[16] Ibid., pp. 160-61.

CHAPTER II

THE "ANAGOGICAL REVELATION"
AND THE CONSTRUCTION OF THE *MOI ANGÉLIQUE*

Thus lyric poetry was abandoned, rejected, for some years. But the *Ego scriptor* must keep on writing; hence another form of "écriture" began in 1894: the *Cahiers* in which Narcissus would record the reflections of his mind for over fifty years, including his farewell to poetry, his flirtations with a new love, Mathematics, and, eventually, his return to the lyric mode. It is in these *Notebooks,* which are the inexhaustible source of so much of Valéry's future poetry, that we will find countless reflections of the Valéryan Angel.

We discussed elsewhere the open-ended and fragmentary nature of much of Valéry's work, the product of a creative technique which precludes a strictly linear or chronological progression in the development of a given theme.[1] That of the Angel is no exception. We can nonetheless trace certain events, noted by the anti-historical Valéry himself — "Je suis anti-historique" (*Cahiers,* XV, 133) — which demonstrate the young poet's predisposition to the angel-archetype, as well as the slow evolution from the Symbolist angel of his early poetry to the very different *moi angélique,* whose presence animates and permeates all of his mature work.

Having followed Valéry's own exposition of his Symbolist literary background as well as the great personal crisis which brought about his break with that tradition, we must now reach forward in time, to *Cahier* entries of the thirties and a prose poem published in 1939 in *Mélange,* for early avatars of Valéry's "angelism."

---

[1] "Structural Variations on a Theme," in *Rhetoric.*

In an entry of 1931 (*Cahiers,* XV, 291), Valéry describes an event of his life, the ceremony in which Maréchal Petain received him, newly-named "Commander," into the Légion d'Honneur at the Invalides (cf. *O,* I, 57). First, he simply describes: "...Pétain me donne l'accolade et me passe au cou sa croix de commandeur - en présence des colonels..." Then the entry continues, after marking other events of the important day:

> ...pauvre chose que l'homo - théorie du Moi pur. . . . - Je conte l'histoire de 'ma petite maison' si moi, si enfantine-ment décisive pour la connaissance de moi - à qui *tout* a tou-jours paru une partie un accident. 'L'Ange' de Degas. A qui les choses et soi, ses idées, ses entours, ses sensations, - ont toujours paru des vêtements - .

Thus, on a day when the celebrated poet receives another public honor, his intimate self, that of the *Cahiers,* returns to origins which explain his insuperable distance from those who celebrate him publicly, and even from that very self that is the public figure. One self beholds the other, the *moi* the "monsieur." Those who knew him best, like Gide and later Degas, called him "Ange," and that sobriquet became Valéry's favorite mask for the self.[2] " 'L'Ange' m'appelait Degas. Il avait plus raison qu'il ne le pouvait croire" (*Cahiers,* XV, 812). The image is thus central to Valéry's immensely complex psyche.

The poet tells the childhood story of "ma petite maison" along with another, "histoire de ma chute," which will later become the prose poem "Enfance aux Cygnes," in a 1935 entry entitled "Mé-moires" (*Cahiers,* XVIII, 218-19):

> Histoire de ma chute dans le bassin au milieu des cygnes et comment soutenu par mes manteau et colerette empesés, toutefois je commençais à couler et avais déjà perdu con-naissance, quand un promeneur étonné de ce cygne qui sombrait, y reconnut un petit enfant, qu'il sauva. À tort ou à raison.

> — Histoire de "Ma petite maison." j'avais peut-être six, peut-être 8 ans. Je me mettais sous les draps, je me retirais

---

[2] Cf. the chapter "Miroir d'un Age" in Nicole Celeyrette-Pietri's mon-umental thesis, *Valéry et le Moi,* pp. 167-73.

la tête les bras de ma longue chemise de nuit, dont je me faisais comme un sac dans lequel je me resserrais comme un fœtus, je me tenais le torse dans les bras — et me répétais: *Ma petite maison ..ma petite maison.*

The first story, as psycho-critical commentators have not failed to note,[3] contains germs of the Narcissus theme, and the second a variation of the "return to the womb" motif. Both of these rare childhood reminiscences reveal a disposition toward the angelic in the Valéryan sense, his insularism; and the poet himself links the "petite maison" souvenir to the angelic self in the 1931 Notebook entry above. Shortly after the 1935 entry, we find on the same page: " - La nuit de Gênes (1892)," which links the decisive turning point of Valéry's youth to those childhood memories.

The story of "ma petite maison," which the poet considers "si enfantinement décisif pour la connaissance de moi," signals not merely a child's *Trieb* to return to the protective womb, but a retreat of a small, vulnerable, and insular self away from the others into the isolation of a construct of his own making, "my little house." This characteristic retreat soon evolves into the adolescent's mental withdrawal from engagement with others, a process recorded many times in the *Notebooks:*

> Je pensais, quand on me grondait, —: ce ne sont que des *associations d'idées,* et je me rehaussais par cette conscience puérile du mécanisme de l'adversaire — que je méprisais dans son autorité, — me donnant la sensation agréable de savoir le regarder comme un animal observé dans sa vie automatique, et moindre que MOI, et *contenu* dans ce regard.

This tactic, by which the youthful persona holds his tormentors — and indeed the entire world — "contenu dans ce regard," is already the favorite Valéryan device of the "regard d'ange." The entry continues:

> Plus tard — peu plus tard — j'ai employé la même défense contre les circonstances ou plutôt contre mes tourments,

---

[3] Cf. Gilberte Aigrisse, *Psychanalyse de Paul Valéry* (Paris: Editions Universitaires, 1964), esp. pp. 20-100, "Monsieur Ange."

> mes obsessions — type d'amour — orgueil — et tout les
> 'sentiments' en général, quand ils devenaient cruels. ... la
> tendance est essentielle en moi. Constante. (*Cahiers,* XVII,
> 224)

In this defensive strategy, Valéry beholds not merely the others, containing them within his "regard," but also, of course, his own *moi* interacting with them. This objective "regard d'ange" always implies a "dédoublement," the division or split, of the self into a beholder and his object, thus linking the figure of the Angel to that of Narcissus: the two selves divided by a mirror.

The angel figure is also frequently associated with the notion of the Fall (cf. the early letter to Gide, "un ange d'or...chu de l'azur facile aux portes de la tombe") from a higher state into an inferior, a human one. Another passage of the *Notebooks,* recalling the same adolescent defense mechanism which we have been describing, emphasizes the sharp separation of the self from the others, who become reified in the process and are reduced to mere robots:

> Ego Le 'psychologue' naissant. Il me souvient, étant encore
> presque enfant, que lorsqu'on me grondait et qu'on s'em-
> portait contre moi, plus la scène durait et le reproche se
> développait, plus je me reprenais et me séparais de l'affaire,
> et regardais la personne en colère comme j'eusse fait un
> phénomène mécanique, un automate dont je prévoyais les
> expressions, les productions d'épithètes et de menaces...
> J'ai toujours eu cette tendance à voir l'automatisme quand
> les hommes passent le point d'indifférence divine et person-
> nifient au lieu de...*phénoménaliser.* Et de même dans les
> amours." (*Cahiers,* XVIII, 784)

The "divine indifference" is the angelic quality par excellence, as Rilke's *Engel* confirm; at the opposite extreme, diametrically opposed to it, is the "personality," which the *Moi pur* must transcend.

We have noted how Valéry employed, though with difficulty, precisely this process of retreat for analysis in his sentimental crisis of the early nineties. By beholding himself, his "personality," as the vulnerable victim of his own sensibilities and imagination, the other, analytic, self at length saved him. Thus the angelic conquered the all too human; and henceforth the emerging *moi* would always be divided into — and torn between — "être" and "connaître," except for very brief periods of harmony, ephemeral returns to Eden: "Ego.

En moi, le contraste de l'intellect et de la sensibilité affective est extrême" (*Cahiers*, XVI, 536).

Numerous entries, like the following from around 1910, express the nostalgia for "ma petite maison": "Souffrance. Je n'ai pas un coin pour être seul, pas une chambre personnelle,... J'envie le prisonnier d'une cellule qui le préserve et qui dans elle est propriétaire du temps, de la solitude, et de la continuité" (*Cahiers*, IV, 367). A similar "Ego" passage, written many years later, recalls another "histoire de ma chute" and its lasting effects: "Je viens de songer à ma nature—à ce qu'elle devait être—...Un incident m'a fait craintif— ...Et il ne m'est resté qu'une espèce de témérité, (jusqu'à la brutalité) intellectuelle. ... Parfois je ressens infiniment que je n'ai rien en commun avec—quoi que ce soit—donc Moi-MÊME" (*Cahiers*, XVI, 541). Both isolation and difference from others, difference even from his own "human self," characterize the angelic self. The importance of the 1892 turning point is repeatedly stressed in the *Notebooks:*

> Ego
> Toute ma "philosophie" est née des efforts et réactions extrêmes qu'excitèrent en moi de 92 à 94, comme défense désespérée,
> 1° l'amour insensé—pour cette dame de R que je n'ai jamais connue que des yeux —
> 2° le désespoir de l'esprit découragé per les perfections *singulières* de Mallarmé et de Rimbaud en 92—brusquement révélées. Et cependant je ne voulais pas faire un poète— mais seulement le *pouvoir de l'être*. C'est le *pouvoir seul* qui m'a toujours fait envie, et non son exercice et l'ouvrage et les resultats extérieurs. C'est bien *moi*—Tout ceci, en présence des 2 ou 3 idées de première valeur que je trouvais dans Poe. (Self-consciousness) ...
> J'ai donc lutté—et me suis consumé—et le résultat fut la bizarre formule: *Tout ceci sont phénomènes mentaux.*
> . . . .
> Trait essentiel de cette époque, Insularismes, despotisme absolu. Rien assez moi, et ce moi — étant une extrême puissance de refus appliqué à tout (*Cahiers*, XXII, pp. 842-43).

Or:

> Mon analytique 1892, produit de la "conscience de soi" appliquée à détruire les obsessions et poisons... Alors, j'ai essayé de *regarder en face* ces poussées, de les réduire à ce

> que la précision de ce regard en faisait—de constituer, en
> somme, un *Moi* dont la douleur fut étrangère, comme la
> *couleur* des choses qu'on voit, et les idées ou images, quasi-
> causes de cette torture, comme les formes des choses qu'on
> voit.
>
> . . . .
>
> Ce fut une période très dure et très féconde—Une lutte
> avec les diables. Nuit de Gênes en octobre '92. (*Cahiers,*
> XXIII, 757-58)

Here, too, the threatened and vulnerable self is distanced from a
hostile world, reducing it — including it/him-self struggling with
its demons — to an object of the angelic transcending vision. In his
old age, Valéry noted: "L'amour de l'époque 92—s'est évanoui—
Mais la formule d'exorcisme par l'intellect s'est fixée et est devenue
un instrument essentiel de ma manière de penser—voilà 50 ans que
je m'y tiens" (*Cahiers,* XXVI, 418).

Thus Valéry insists repeatedly on the significance of that "amour
insensé" which did so much to determine his destiny, as well as on
the temper of mind which produced his particular resolution of the
crisis: the construction of the angelic self, whose reflections were to
appear later in numerous heroes of his poetic universe: Teste, for
example, Gladiator, Descartes or Leonardo, Sémiramis, and finally
"mon Faust." But throughout Valéry's life, the angelic self is ever
threatened by its human image, its other self, its participation in the
animal, in the unending recurrence and repetition of the material
world. Narcissus' self is divided, and the beautiful image is as fragile
as the moi that projects it. Teste, "le maître de sa pensée," who is
"dur comme un ange," his maker tells us, "ne pourrait se prolonger
dans le réel pendant plus de quelques quarts d'heure" (*O,* II, 13).

A Notebook entry from the early twenties again recalls the "coup
d'état of 1892, which signaled the victory of the angelic intelligence,
but this time along with another event, of 1920, that almost destroyed that victory: "Si je me regarde historiquement," writes the
fifty-two-year-old Valéry, "je trouve deux événements formidables
dans ma vie secrète. Un coup d'état en 92 et quelque chose d'immense, d'illimité d'incommensurable en 1920. J'ai lancé la foudre
sur ce que j'étais en 92. 28 ans après, elle est tombée sur moi de
très loin" (*Cahiers,* VIII, 762). The second "event" is another "crise
sentimentale." Now a mature and profound love for the woman
discreetly referred to as "Béatrice" or "K" (the poetess Catherine

Pozzi) in the *Notebooks* threatens to overwhelm and annihilate the angelic intelligence constructed in youth and cultivated for over twenty years by the *Moi pur*.

Peter Kunze stresses the capital importance of the event of 1920 in the evolution of the mythopoetic figure in Valéry's later work; [4] and we agree with that position insofar as, in a sense, all of Valéry's *œuvre* is "autobiographical." Has he not told us himself that even his two great lyric poems are autobiographical? Commenting on "La Jeune Parque," he says: "Qui saura me lire, lira une autobiographie, dans la forme" (*O*, I, 1622); and about "Le Cimetière marin," the poet says: "...le poème..fut un monologue de 'moi', dans lequel les thèmes les plus simples et les plus constants de ma vie affective et intellectuelle...fussent appelés, tramés, opposés..." (*O*, I, 1503). Here the accent is again on the "affective" and the "intellectual" and their "opposition." Thus, in 1920, love threatened the Angel; but the angelic self had always lived precariously dependent on the other, the human one. From the outset, Narcissus is divided into an affective and an intellectual *moi*, the latter — "l'esprit pur" — observing the former, "ce beau reflet des désordres humains" (*O*, I, 123). Either of the two dissenting halves, moreover, may equally threaten the One-self, for whom the "tentation de l'esprit" can become at least as dangerous as that of the flesh. [5]

Valéry once wrote "An Abstract Tale" about these two selves — and a third who observes them — entitled "La Révélation anagogique," which became the last of the *Histoires brisées* (*O*, II, 466-67) published posthumously. [6] The earlier and somewhat longer version of the tale is a *Notebook* entry of 1938; both versions are dated "MDCCCXCII" in the text. It is a literary, i.e., mythologized and symbolic, transformation of the 1892 experience and its consequences. Here the poet is concerned not merely with the self, or a rebellious half of the *moi;* rather he sees its two warring factions figured as "two terrible angels," against each of which the *moi* must

[4] Peter Kunze, unpublished thesis on "Le Mythe de l'Ange dans l'œuvre de Paul Valéry" (thèse de 3° cycle, présentée à l'Université de Clermont II, U.E.R. Lettres, soutenue le 20 mars 1978).

[5] Cf. Marcel Raymond, *Paul Valéry et la tentation de l'esprit* (Neuchatel: A la Baconniere, 1948).

[6] Gallimard, 1950.

defend itself. The "Anagogical Revelation" is a Valéryan version of the Biblical tale of Jacob's Struggle with the Angel, which object-ifies and symbolizes an inner victory of the self over it(s)self(ves), a commemoration of the battle and the victory of 1892:

An Abstract Tale—

La Révélation anagogique

1) En ce temps-là (MDCCCXCII) il me fut révélé par deux terribles anges Nous et Eros l'existence d'une voie de destruction et de domination, et d'une Limite certaine à l'extrême de cette voie. Je connus la certitude de la Borne et l'importance de la connaître: ce qui est d'un intérêt com-parable à celui de la connaissance du Solide — ou (autre-ment symbolisé) d'un usage analogue à celui du mur contre lequel le combattant adossé et ne redoutant nulle attaque *a tergo,* peut faire face à tous ses adversaires également *affrontés,* et PAR LÀ, RENDUS COMPARABLES EN-TR'EUX — (ceci étant le point le plus remarquable de cette découverte, — car parmi ces adversaires, *Celui qui est Soi,* ou ceux qui sont la *Personne* qu'on est et ses diverses insuf-fisances, figurent comme les étrangères et adventices cir-constances).

Et les deux anges eux-mêmes me chassant devant eux, se fondaient donc en un seul: — et moi, me retournant vers et contre eux, je ne combattais qu'une seule puissance, une fois le Mur ressenti aux épaules.

2) J'ai cherché à voir cette borne — et à définir ce mur. — J'ai voulu "écrire" pour moi, et en moi, pour me servir de cette connaissance, les conditions de limite ou fermeture, ou (ce qui revient au même) celles d'unification de tout ce qui vient s'y heurter .... la pensée se fait des domaines illusoires situés au delà de la Borne — soit que le Mur se comporte comme un miroir, soit comme une glace transpa-rente — ce que je ne crois pas. Miroir plutôt; ....

Que si cependant tu étudies ce que tu y vois, tu obser-veras que le personnage étranger fait ce que tu te sens faire.

Ce sont donc les variations corrélatives qui te permet-tront de comprendre que ce personnage est *de toi*—; qu'il n'a pas un *acte* de plus que *Toi*;

et par là aussi, ce Toi prend place en quelque manière dans l'*Antégo,* et devient partie.

3) Ainsi des propriétés de topologie, de limitation, de com-mune-quasi-mesure, m'apparaissaient—et me dirigeaient vers un système de notation *absolue*—qui excluait l'explication —pour tenter la représentation utilisable—et la possibilité de traduire en pouvoirs réels toute chose—

4) Ainsi une volonté de pousser la *fonction du Moi* à l'extrême—et non sa personnalisation croissante .... (*Cahiers,* XXI, 70-72).

The editors of the English translation of the text suggest that the title might have been inspired by Baudelaire's "Révélation magnétique," translation of Poe's "Mesmeric Revelation," which would then also explain the English epigraph, "An Abstract Tale," as an allusion to Poe.[7] The term "anagogical," moreover, alludes, through its exegetical overtones, to Jacob's Struggle with the Angel. The "anagogical" level of the traditional fourfold interpretation of Scripture pointed to an ultimate or mystical meaning. Poe's "Mesmeric Revelation" is a pseudo-philosophical speculation about the nature of material and spiritual substance, revealed by a mesmerized subject as he passes from the living to the dead. Poe's "abstract" speculations, with their pseudo-scientific flavor, had always fascinated Valéry. Baudelaire's heirs, including Valéry, had admired in Poe above all the aesthetician and theoretician: "Poe le premier," says Valéry, "a songé à donner un fondement théorique pur aux ouvrages," adding, "Mallarmé et moi-même" (*Cahiers,* XII, 703).[8] From the earliest references to Poe, we saw the young poet's fascination with "des doctrines savantes du grand Edgar Allan Poe," who "précise l'écho mystérieux des choses...aussi certain qu'un rapport mathématique."

Thus Poe had been directive for Valéry from the beginning, not as poet but as speculative theoretician of both the arts and the sciences. The "Anagogical Revelation" records the important turn-

---

[7] Paul Valéry, *Poems in the Rough,* Vol. 2, Bollingen Series XLV (Princeton: Princeton University Press, 1969), p. 311.

[8] We share Edouard Gaède's amazement at how a text like "Eureka," that eclectic *vulgarisation* of diverse theories on "The Material and Spiritual Universe," labeled "A Prose Poem," could have so profoundly contributed to Valéry's turning from poetry to science (cf. Gaède, *Nietzsche et Valéry* [Paris: Gallimard, 1962], esp. pp. 55ff.). About the impact of "Eureka" on the construction of the new self after 1892 there is no doubt. In a letter to Gide of 1892, from which we have quoted above, Valéry writes: "Je suis au fond d'*Eureka*" (*Correspondance,* p. 150). And in "Au Sujet d'*Eureka,*" an essay first published in 1921, and then several times subsequently, Valéry recalls: "ces sciences, si froidement enseignées, ont été fondées et accrues par des hommes qui y mettaient un intérêt passionné. *Eureka* me fit sentir quelque chose de cette passion" (*O,* I, p. 856).

ing point in that "comédie intellectuelle" which is Valéry's great
sub-text, the "deep structure" of which all his subsequent writings
are the transformations, and whose hero is the angelic self, whether
he bears the mask of a Teste, a Leonardo, or Sémiramis, or Faust.
The "revelation" itself is that of the "abstract," analytic and scientific method — that of the Angel — by which those other powers,
the evil angels Eros *and* Nous who fuse into one "Anti-ego" threaten-
ing the *moi,* can be overcome. Nicole Celeyrette-Pietri, in her analysis
of the strategies of the Valéryan *Moi,* finds that "le 'Conte abstrait'
...raconte l'invention du Système, entendu comme *réduction* à l'Absolu." [9] That "système absolu" to which Valéry aspired is a scientific-
mathematical one which would preoccupy him for many years while
he abandoned lyric poetry; and it was, paradoxically, inspired by a
poet: Edgar Allan Poe, whom Mallarmé had imaged as an Angel
with the naked sword.

The "Anagogical Revelation" personifies *Nous* and *Eros,* marking
the division between *esprit* and *corps* which is a constant in Valéry,
who remained essentially a Cartesian dualist all his life. *Nous,* the
mind and reason, was for the Greeks an intelligent purposive principle of the world, and for the neo-Platonists the first emanation
of God, while Eros was already a Greek mythological figure in
Hesiod's time, and continues to symbolize the pleasure-directed life
instincts whose energy is derived from the libido. Throughout the
Notebooks, Valéry refers to the "psychic" and mental with the
Greek letter psi; to the "physical" and sensorial with the letter phi.
An entry of the thirties notes, for example, that "le plus *réel* et le
plus important problème de la connaissance est pour moi celui de la
distinction et des rapports entre les deux faces de la connaissance, le
sensible et le psychique. ... φ et ψ —ma première pensée fut de les
considérer en concurrence—comme des termes qui se limitent réci-
proquement. $\varphi + \psi = C$ (*Cahiers,* XVIII, p. 887).

We remarked that Valéry remained essentially a Cartesian dualist; he admired in Descartes, "ce grand capitaine de l'esprit," another
intellectual hero and angelic self, and his admiration for this "mag-
nifique et mémorable Moi" is expressed in the five essays on the
philosopher, published between 1926 and 1943 (cf. *O,* I, 787-854).

---

[9] Celeyrette-Pietri, *Valéry et le Moi,* p. 710.

Descartes' *Method,* along with certain ideas of Poe, influenced the young Valéry's search for a "method" of his own; and the figure of Descartes contributed to that of Teste. In an 1894 letter to Gide, Valéry writes: "j'ai relu *Le Discours de la Méthode* tantôt, c'est bien le roman moderne, comme il pourrait être fait. ... c'est le point à reprendre et il faudra donc écrire la vie d'une théorie comme on a trop écrit celle d'une passion." [10] Descartes had mastered the world by quantifying it; the young Valéry wants to master his world by a "Universal Arithmetic," a "Method" he discusses in letters of the 1890s to his friend Gustave Fourment:

> En somme je ne fais d'autres postulats généraux que ceux des mathématiques, et il faut bien en passer par là, ou s'asseoir. Je me permets, alors, des *constructions* comme on dit en *géométrie.* Au fond tout mon truc est là. Je crois énormément à la richesse de ce procédé qui passe par l'arbitraire et arrive à la démonstration. [11]

This is clearly the "système de notation *absolue*—qui excluait l'explication—pour tenter la représentation utilisable—et la possibilité de traduire en pouvoirs réels toute chose" of the "Anagogical Revelation." In another letter to the same friend, Valéry calls it his "Universal Arithmetic" and explains:

> Mais passons au point de vue important. Celui d'*Arithmetica universalis.* Je ne considère pas les états mentaux en eux-mêmes; ils sont infinis, discontinus, etc. Mais il est possible de croire que leurs variations ou leur sort ne soit susceptible d'être mieux connu. Ainsi, la géométrie euclidienne ne décrit pas les formes réelles... [12]

Nicole Celeyrette-Pietri has discussed extensively Valéry's "Fascination Mathématique," the construction and the ultimate failure of the "universal arithmetic," and his preoccupation with an "algèbre du moi." [13] If the "système *absolu*" ultimately proved a failure, Valéry nevertheless continued to lean on scientific models in his

---

[10] *Gide-Valéry Correspondance,* p. 213.
[11] *Valéry-Fourment Correspondance,* p. 142.
[12] Ibid., pp. 146-47.
[13] Celeyrette-Pietri, *Valéry et le Moi,* pp. 9-75.

unceasing exploration of the human psyche. He had a special predilection for the phases of thermodynamic systems; an entry of his
later years, in the 1940s when the "universal arithmetic" had long
since been abandoned, reads: "Ego $\varphi \psi$ Phases. Ma meilleure idée
—fut celle de *phases*—[nom que j'ai pris par vague analogie à la
terminologie de Gibbs]" (*Cahiers*, XXIII, 663). Judith Robinson
explains how "dans sa recherce d'un genre de mathématique qui pût
convenir à l'analyse de l'esprit, Valéry était très influencé par l'exemple de la thermodynamique." [14]

The other great revelation of the "Abstract Tale" is that of the
"Limite certaine" which Valéry's persona — the self struggling with
the angels — likens to the Solid underfoot, or that wall against which
the fighter sets his back as he fights off the assaults of the adversary
— *Nous* and *Eros,* now fused into one "Antégo." Of that Limit, the
persona coments: "Je connus la certitude de la Borne et l'importance
de la connaître." Ned Bastet has analyzed this notion of the limit,
which Valéry takes up repeatedly in the *Notebooks.* [15] There is a
limit beyond which the terrible angels *Nous* and *Eros,* powerful
like gods — for we recognize in the extremes of ψ and φ Nietzsche's
warring Apollonian and Dionysian halves of man's tragic psyche —
cannot drive their victim. The angels may well have chased man from
Paradise, but after his Fall from Eden, man found something new,
a new refuge and a limit, beyond all torture: Death, that other side
of life on earth, unknown in heaven.

After the Night in which he saw the great Limit, the "Boundary
at the far end," Valéry repeatedly flirted with that "extreme point,"
like the moth with the flame, like Teste praying, "donnez, ô Noir,
—donnez la suprême pensée..." "Quelle tentation, pourtant, que la
mort," muses Teste, "une chose inimaginable et qui se met dans
l'esprit sous les formes du désir et de l'horreur tour à tour" (*O,* II,
37, 75). With that solid wall *a tergo,* the *moi* can face any adversary;
for it supports and it attracts; backed up against it, man defies the
gods.

---

[14] Robinson, *L'Analyse de l'esprit,* pp. 64ff.
[15] Ned Bastet, "L'Expérience de la Borne et du Dépassement chez Valéry"
in *Cahiers Paul Valéry I: Poétique et poésie* (Paris: Gallimard, 1975), pp.
57-90.

Some of Valéry's heroes — Teste, Narcissus, Sémiramis, Faust — like Hölderlin's Empedocles, accomplish the leap. The ways of both *Nous* and *Eros* come together at the limit, when the self, rather than falling as their victim, becomes their master, both comprehends and accepts that at the extreme point of "l'esprit," as at the extreme point of desire, lies Nothingness — "la pureté du Non-être." "Ainsi sur la voie de la Connaissance," comments Bastet, "comme sur celle de l'Amour, c'est la Mort qui apparaît comme l'essence dernière de la Borne—ou plutôt comme ce qui la supprime si l'on ose pénétrer dans le foyer de la destruction." [16]

The persona of the "Révélation anagogique" is a third, analytic, self who separates himself from the other two — "*celui qui est Soi, ou ceux qui sont la Personne qu'on est*" — to observe them and the Wall, that is his own limits. We recognize in this persona not merely Narcissus, but the *moi angélique* who, after defending the vulnerable "person" that he is, rejects and transcends that lesser self.

---

[16] Ibid., p. 85.

CHAPTER III

TESTE, AGATHE, AND "L'ANGE LIONARDO"

A Valéryan hero who did indeed overcome the "person" in himself is Monsieur Teste who "avait *tué la marionnette*" (*O*, II, 17). Valéry never forgot, moreover, that "Borne" discovered in 1892; in one of Valéry-Teste's posthumously published "Pensées," the persona relates: "je ne suis pas tourné du côté du monde. J'ai le visage vers le MUR. Pas un rien de la surface du mur qui me soit inconnu" (*O*, II, 72). Teste is one of the great angelic figures of Valéry's "Comedy of the Intellect," an abstraction that, as its creator remarked, could not exist in the concrete. What Angel can?

Valéry's preoccupation with Teste began in 1894-95, again under the inspiration of Poe. In a letter to Mallarmé's commentator, Albert Thibaudet, he writes in 1912: "M. Teste n'a pas de rapport que j'aie voulu avec Mallarmé. C'est un récit, comme tous les miens, de circonstance. Avec des notes vite assemblées, j'ai fait ce faux portrait de personne; caricature, si vous voulez, d'un être qu'aurait dû faire vivre—encore Poe"; [1] and Jean Prévost recalls a conversation with Valéry in which the poet told him that "la lecture d'Edgard [sic] Poe et surtout le personnage de Dupin avait été le point de départ pour imaginer M. Teste..." (*O*, II, 1380). Valéry tells us that "Teste... est un personnage obtenu par le fractionnement d'un être réel dont on extrairait les moments les plus intellectuels pour en composer le tout de la vie d'un personnage imaginaire" (*O*, II, 1381); and this fragmentary nature of the persona is reflected in the form of that "roman moderne," the fragments — letters, "ex-

---

[1] Valéry, *Lettres à quelques-uns*, pp. 97-98.

traits du log-book," dialogues, sketches and "pensées" — that make up the "Cycle Teste." It preoccupied Valéry from his twenty-third year to the end of his life, when he "avait, avant sa mort, réuni un ensemble de notes et d'esquisses avec l'intention de les utiliser pour une nouvelle édition de M. Teste" (*O, II, 56*). The nucleus of the Teste fragments is one of Valéry's most celebrated texts, "La Soirée avec Monsieur Teste," first published in *Le Centaure* in 1896. In a letter of that year he writes to Gide: "je bafouille de plus en plus avec M. Teste. Je suis aussi désarmé que possible... Tu tiendras compte de ce que c'est mon premier essai d'un bonhomme, etc. Genre roman (sans intrigue)." [2]

Teste's name means "witness," for he has developed a vision that distances him from both the world and from himself, reducing them to mere objects of his mind's eye, his consciousness: "M. Teste est le témoin ... Conscious—Teste, Testis" [lat. "one who attests"] (*O, II, 64*). His name, moreover, echoes "tête," appropriate for this "monstre" of the intellect. Teste is as "unnatural" as an angel; and his most angelic trait is his "regard." It is this "regard" which is most thoroughly analyzed in "La Soirée avec Monsieur Teste." Its epigraph reads "*Vita Cartesii est simplicissima...*," and its persona, Cartesian himself, relates how he met Teste in October of 1893, and how, after much thought, he came to believe that "M. Teste had managed to discover laws of the mind of which we know nothing" (*O, II, 17*). He adds, "je sentais qu'il était le maître de sa pensée; j'écris là cette absurdité" (*O, II, 18*). This mastery gave Teste super-human—angelic—power, for, "s'il eût tourné contre le monde la puissance régulière de son esprit, rien ne lui eût résisté" (*O, II, 19*). Teste, however, is the man of the "possible," of potency rather than act; a *Notebook* entry reads: "M. Teste dit: Mon possible ne m'abandonne jamais" (*Cahiers*, X, 357). He does not *need* to exercise his latent strength: "Mr. Teste est-il autre chose que le possible, l'incarnation du possible en tant que—nous en usons et disposons? Et ce possible-là, est-ce pas—ce que l'on entend par intellectuel" (*Cahiers*, XI, 768)? Teste did not commit the error which is every great man's flaw: to manifest, to reveal, himself. For he is one of those rare geniuses who sees all without being seen, who reduces

---

[2] *Gide-Valéry, Correspondance,* p. 275.

the world to an object without being object for another. He is himself the object of his vision, while escaping that of the others. When Valéry tries to give us "Un Portrait de Monsieur Teste," he concludes: "Il n'y pas d'image certaine de M. Teste. Tous les portraits diffèrent les uns des autres" (*O*, II, 63); the persona of "La Soirée" tries to make himself the witness of this witness who seems to escape him, but admits, "je simplifie grossièrement des propriétés impénétrables" (*O*, II, 19); and in another fragment, Teste warns his interlocutor, "ne me comparez pas à d'autres: car, primo vous ne me connaissez pas,—et puis, vous ne connaissez pas les autres" (*O*, II, 61). Does not Teste "escape" even his own wife? Émilie Teste writes: "Il faut l'avoir vu dans ces excès d'absence! Alors sa physionomie s'altère,—s'efface! ...Un peu plus de cette absorption, et je suis sûre qu'il se rendrait invisible..." (*O*, II, 30)!

The highlight of the "Soirée" is "Teste au théâtre," in which the persona recalls how, exactly "two years and three months ago this evening," he had accompanied his friend to the theatre, a veritable feast of the "regard." For as the eyes of the audience are captured by the scene, Teste beholds that audience, while the persona watches Teste (watching the others, watching the performance), the spectators thus constituting the spectacle for the narrator and Teste. The latter comments: " 'le suprême *les* simplifie' ... Il ajouta, 'L'éclairage les tient.' Je dis en riant: 'Vous aussi?' Il répondit: 'Vous aussi' " (*O*, II, 21). But that "regard" which reduces the others to mere objects includes, as we have said, the *moi* in the objectification.

After the theatre, the persona accompanies Teste home, to a room which in its cold impersonality resembles Igitur's midnight chamber: "c'était le logis quelconque, analogue au point quelconque des théorèmes" (*O*, II, 23). Teste suffers, and after a cigar with his friend, lies down on his bed, analyzing "cette géométrie de ma souffrance," the phenomenon which reminds the head of its body, where φ and ψ intersect. Here Teste's powers feel their limitation: "Que peut un homme? Je combats tout,—hors la souffrance de mon corps, au delà d'une certaine grandeur. C'est là, pourtant, que je devrais commencer. Car, souffrir, c'est donner à quelque chose une attention suprême, et je suis un peu l'homme de l'attention..." (*O*, II, 25). Teste had, of course, fore-*seen* his illness, as well as his death: "je crois que cette vue sur une portion évidente de l'avenir devrait

faire partie de l'éducation" (*O*, II, 25). For nothing should escape
his view, neither the others, nor the self — and its Limit. The
"Soirée" closes with Teste finally disappearing — into sleep, i.e.,
absence — after his introspection has removed him to an extreme
point, a limit beyond which Narcissus cannot see: "je suis étant, et
me voyant; me voyant me voir, et ainsi de suite..." (*O*, II, 25).

This ultimate degree of inner vision, of intro-spection, of "Self-
consciousness" — one of his favorite words, inherited from Poe —
fascinated Valéry all his life. It underlies not merely his "Narcisse"
poems, but the other great lyric and prose compositions as well.
The "Jeune Parque," for example, says: "Je me voyais me voir,
sinueuse, et dorais / De regards en regards, mes profondes forêts"
(*O*, I, 97); and the theme of the prose poem "Sur la Place publique"
is "celui qui se sent voir ce qu'il voit," where the subject's successive
retreats from himself, in order to behold himself as object, attain a
limit beyond which he cannot recede: "je suis donc à l'extrémité de
quelque puissance; et il n'y a plus de place dans mon esprit pour un
peu plus d'esprit" (*O*, II, 689). Teste is the hero of that "regard"
and this "esprit," angelic traits both; and in a Notebook entry from
1944, Valéry records: "le: *Je pense que je pense*... s'arrête, ou se
perd en lui-même dès après la seconde application du signe: *Je pense
que*.. ψ (ψ (ψ ...). Je puis *écrire* ψ (ψ ... avec la liberté de l'algèbre.
Mais cette écriture est vaine, nonsens, ne représente rien.— ...(Mon-
sieur Teste seul s'élevait parfois pendant un instant au 3me degré—
etc.)" (*Cahiers*, XXVIII, 248).

Teste was capable of this mental gymnastics, and of the refinement of external objects, of phenomena, into the purely mathematical, since, except for moments of physical pain (and we have noted
that he even *envisioned* these), and for moments of love,[3] he was
virtually all "esprit" and intellect, a *Moi pur*. He speaks, for example,
of money: "huit cent dix millions soixante quinze mille cinq cent
cinquante... J'écoutais cette musique inouïe sans suivre le calcul"
(*O*, II, 23). Now the purity of the *Moi pur* meant for Valéry the
separation of the mental from the physical. We noted that he remained essentially a dualist; and his playful variation of the *cogito*,
"Variations sur Descartes: Parfois je pense; et parfois, je suis,"

---

[3] Cf. the "Lettre de Madame Émilie Teste" (*O*, II, 26-36).

reveals that fundamental disposition. Or consider: "—Bien (dit Mr. Teste). L'essentiel est contre la vie" (*Cahiers,* XVII, 438). The *Moi pur* is by definition "inhuman," for the human is precisely that impure *mélange* of the body and the mind. In one of the "Pensées" of *Tel quel,* significantly entitled "Deux," Valéry reflects: "L'homme devint aussi pur que l'ange ou que l'animal; car l'impureté n'est que le mélange des natures. Fatigué de n'être ni ange ni bête, il se résolut à être tantôt l'un tantôt l'autre; tantôt 'corps' et tantôt 'esprit'" (O, II, 344). Elsewhere in the *Notebooks,* he says: "J'ai de la répugnance pour tout ce qui est mélange désordonné d'animal et d'ange. Mais j'aime l'un et l'autre bien séparés" (*Cahiers,* XIV, 354). This stance is further reflected in the "Paraboles" of 1935.

That this *Moi pur* rejects the "person" who he is and who reduces him to a mere "semblable" is only logical; thus Mme Teste's spiritual advisor finds her husband "un monstre d'isolement et de connaissance singulière" (O, II, 35). A *Cahier* entry from the 1940s reads:

> Teste—L'homme 'intelligent' répugne à se sentir une personne, un *monsieur,* bien défini, et cependant tient à être *Soi!* Il veut et ne veut pas être quelqu'un. Il veut *être quelqu'un* par passion de se distinguer des autres— *Ne pas l'être* par horreur de leur ressembler ... lui qui veut les rendre *tous* inutiles, moins que lui—puisqu'il les 'comprend', les absorbe ou résume—et les surpasse et annule! —et qui se sent, se croit *capable* d'eux tous. (*Cahiers,* XXVI, 288)

We recall "Teste au théâtre" and seem to detect here a certain Nietzschean strain. The "Übermensch" and Valéry's Angel have some traits in common, for both ideal figures aspire after a *Macht* or "pouvoir" which could elevate them beyond the human.

"Que peut un homme?" is Teste's leitmotif; an entry of the 40s reads: "Poter—Ego Mon 'Cogito'—Il est inscrit dans la *Soirée avec M. Teste*— —'Que peut un homme?'" (*Cahiers,* XXIV, 595). We need quote no further: "what is man's potential?" is the leitmotif of Valéry's life.

Teste, then, is one of Valéry's great angelic heroes, a celebration of the *Moi pur* which culminates in the image of "The Man of Glass," the *moi* become a pure crystal of lucidity:

L'Homme de verre

> ...Si droite est ma vision, si pure ma sensation, si maladroi-
> tement complète ma connaissance, et si déliée, si nette ma
> représentation, et ma science si achevée que je me pénètre
> depuis l'extrémité du monde jusqu'à ma parole silencieuse;
> et de l'informe *chose* qu'on désire se levant, le long de fibres
> connues et de centres ordonnés, je me *suis,* je me réponds,
> je me reflète et me répercute, je frémis à l'infini des miroirs
> —je suis de verre. (*O,* II, 44)

The persona of the *Notebook* muses:

> ...Te rappelles-tu le temps où tu étais ange? Ange sans
> Christ, je me souviens. C'était une affaire de regard et de
> volonté, l'idée de tout traverser avec mes yeux. Je n'aimais
> que le feu. Je croyais que rien à la fin ne résisterait à mon
> regard... C'est exagérer la distance infinie qu'il y a entre
> *moi* et les autres, entre tout moi et tous les autres."
> (*Cahiers,* IV, 705)

Closely related to Teste is the figure of "Agathe" (*O,* II, 1388-
92), Teste's nocturnal sister, and heroine of a fragment that was
published only posthumously. [4] In a previous discussion of this text, [5]
we suggested why Valéry might have chosen not to "finish," nor
publish "Agathe." He first mentions the project in a letter to Gide
of January 1898, predicting even then that it would be too difficult
to finish, for this projected exploration of the functioning and gradual alterations of the mind as it falls into sleep and dream is "fort
dur à même envisager." In a later discussion, various titles appear;
and Jean Levaillant found in the early drafts a "Nocturne selon
M. Teste." [6] The card inserted in the posthumous luxury edition
of 1956 states: "L'auteur a parfois songé à lui donner un autre titre,
inspiré d'Edgar Poe, *Manuscrit trouvé dans une cervelle* que portent
certains brouillons."

---

[4] Paul Valéry, *Agathe* (Paris: 1956). Cf. Nicole Celeyrette-Pietri, "*Agathe*"
ou "*Le Manuscrit trouvé dans une cervelle*": genèse et exégèse d'un conte de
l'entendement (Paris: Lettres modernes, 1981).

[5] "The White Night of *Agathe:* A Fragment by Paul Valéry," in *Essays
in French Literature,* 12 (November, 1975), 37-58.

[6] Jean Levaillant, *La Jeune Parque et poèmes en prose* (Paris: Gallimard,
1974), p. 166.

"Agathe," first conceived as a "conte," [7] was soon envisaged as a fragment. When Gide wrote to Valéry in order to solicit a book on behalf of Gallimard in 1912, Valéry proposed "un volume très rompu—prose, vers assez mêlés—comme un cahier...je pourais alors, s'il plaît au temps, tripatouiller *Monsieur Teste* ainsi: 1° La Soirée; 2° L'excommencement d'*Agathe* qui ferait l'intérieur de la nuit de M. Teste." [8] Maurice Toesca relates a conversation with Valéry around 1944, according to which *La Soirée avec Monsieur Teste* was to become part of the great work, that *roman d'un cerveau* to which Valéry alludes elsewhere, [9] and of which the "Manuscrit trouvé dans une cervelle" was to become a chapter. [10]

In the Teste cycle, "Agathe" was to become a fragment of the night of the hero—"moi qui adore la navigation de la nuit" (*O,* II, p. 24). And in "Agathe," Teste is no longer mirrored by the observations of the others, like the acquaintance of the café or his wife Émilie; rather he becomes himself the witness and mirror of his changing states of mind and being. For during his night, Teste is alone; his friend, the persona of the "Soirée," was leaving him as he appeared to be going to sleep, murmuring, "je suis étant, et me voyant; me voyant me voir, et ainsi de suite..." "Agathe" becomes the poetic mono-dialogue of a mind beholding itself think, and therefore speak, during the fragment of a night. [11]

Valéry, as we noted, saw the "fonctionnement" of the mind in terms of phases which he liked to compare to those of a closed

---

[7] Octave Nadal, *A Mesure haute* (Paris: Mercure de France, 1964), pp. 240-41.

[8] *Gide-Valéry, Correspondance,* pp. 426-27.

[9] For example, "Je voyais en lui [Leonardo] le personnage principal de cette Comédie Intellectuelle qui n'a pas jusqu'ici rencontré son poète, et qui serait pour mon goût bien plus précieuse encore que *La Comédie humaine,* et même que *La Divine Comédie*" ("Note et digression," *O,* I, 1201).

[10] Maurice Toesca, "Paul Valéry: Agathe" in *La Nouvelle Revue Française* (mai 1957), 910-11.

[11] "Le thème du poème," as the commentary accompanying the text displayed at the 1971 Valéry exposition at the Bibliothèque Nationale states, "s'apparente à celui de *La Jeune Parque:* sous une forme ou autre c'est toujours repris inlassablement le même drame de l'esprit" (*Paul Valéry Exposition du Centenaire,* Bibliothèque Nationale, Paris: 1971), pp. 126-27. It is, indeed, "always the same drama of the mind" that Valéry recreates for us, that of Narcissus whose double self, a consciousness beholding itself, a self-consciousness, is both "regard" and reflection.

thermodynamic system, and these transformations from phase to phase fascinated him particularly when he observed not merely different thoughts, but different states of mind succeed one another, such as wakefulness followed by sleep, or the drifting inattentiveness of the mind followed by its alert phase. In "Agathe" one follows the mind's cyclical progression from phase to phase, from wakefulness to sleep and dream, to awakening, to thinking, with a mind-persona — a variation of the *Moi pur* — who thinks, that is verbalizes, and sometimes writes, his experience. The text is composed of eleven major sections of varying length, each marking a phase of internal time. From the first to the fifth section, the persona withdraws deeper and deeper into sleep and night. Then in the middle of that section, which constitutes the center of the poem, this regression is reversed as the *moi* awakens fully, to become progressively more lucid. The cyclical rising mental action then comes to a culmination in the tenth section, while the final one marks the falling off, the denouement, of this drama of the mind.

We will not follow "Agathe" through these phases of her nocturnal voyage, but meet her at the poem's climax, when that mind stands motionless, her voyage arrested, as she invents and discovers

> les effets de quelque créature extrêmement désirée de l'esprit; vue une fois, elle absorberait dans une fixité splendide n'importe quelle pensée pouvant venir après. (*O*, II, 1392)

And this "creature extremely desired by the mind" is that "supreme thought," the object of Teste's prayer: "Donnez, ô Noir,—donnez la suprême pensée" (*O*, II, 37). Agathe, "dans cette enveloppe parfaite nocturne" in her "sphère unique," feels so close to her ideal that she is already touching its laws. And as she is observing the movement of her thoughts, "chaque pensée se module, tourne en observation d'elle-même, trainant une valeur après soi" (*O*, II, 1392). In the solitary stillness of her night, Agathe is all thinking, and her mind, "une limpidité identique," is a transparent mirror in which she sees the functioning of "les plus profondes déductions, les visites les plus internes."

If this crystal were always completely clear, "si toujours cette pureté se pouvait," the intellect would be so lucid as to be a transparent and necessary system, "permettant la séparation de ses as-

pects, et la division de la durée spirituelle en intervalles clairs . . . .
bientôt, je ferais toutes mes idées irréductibles ou confondues." This
ideal already foreshadows Valéry's last poem, whose beginnings go
back to the twenties, the prose poem "L'Ange," which opens:

> Une manière d'ange était assis sur le bord d'une fontaine.
> Il s'y mirait, et se voyait Homme...
>
> . . . .
>
> Et il s'interrogeait dans l'univers de sa substance spirituelle
> merveilleusement pure, où toutes les idées vivaient égale-
> ment entre elles et de lui-même et dans une telle perfection
> de leur harmonie et promptitude de leurs correspondances,
> qu'on eût dit qu'il eût pu s'évanouir, et le système étince-
> lant comme un diadème, de leur nécessité simultanée sub-
> sister par soi seul dans sa sublime plénitude. (*O*, I, 205-6)

At the zenith of its concentration, "Agathe's" *Moi pur* as well as
the poetic text in which it is embedded, attains the climax: "vo-
luptueusement, la palpitation de l'espace multiple ne ravive plus
qu'à peine ma chair"; Agathe, approaching the pure "Zéro," is all
mind, and her mind is a virtual system, a spiritual *diadème,* independent of its content as well as of any particular existence: it has
attained the Absolute of the Angel:

> L'ensemble de connaissances diverses, également imminen-
> tes, qui me constitue, ...forme maintenant *un système nul
> ou indifférent à ce qu'il vient de produire ou approfondir,*
> quand l'ombre imaginaire doucement cède à toute naissance,
> et c'est l'esprit. (*O*, II, 1392) [my italics]

But then, after the rising action of this dramatic voyage of the mind
through the night, its cyclical progression leading up to the final
ascent and hybris of its angelic culmination, there comes a "falling
off," the sinking of the ship, and, as Mallarmé had once expressed
it most profoundly, "RIEN de la mémorable crise...N'AURA EU
LIEU...QUE LE LIEU". [12]

The poem's denouement reflects what Valéry had frequently expressed in the *Notebooks,* that "toute puissance spirituelle est fondée

---

[12] Stéphane Mallarmé, *Œuvres complètes* (Paris: Gallimard, 1945), pp.
474-75.

sur les innombrables hasards de la pensée" (*Cahiers*, IV, 728). Agathe
— Teste — that mind witnessing its own mutations and the birth
and the death of its creatures, cannot understand her mystery, just
as the Angel who "pendant une éternité... ne cessa de connaître et
de ne pas comprendre" (*O*, I, 206).

Another of Valéry's heroes of the intellect — "le personnage
principal de cette Comédie Intellectuelle qui n'a jusqu'ici rencontré
son poète" — is his Leonardo da Vinci, who first appeared in an
article in *La Nouvelle Revue* in 1895, under the title "Introduction
à la Méthode de Léonard de Vinci." Like so much of Valéry's work,
it was written "sur commande," and in a letter to Gide, early that
year, Valéry writes: "Je travaille sans enthousiasme à mon article
et il neige .... Ça sera écrit sans soleil et sans envie .... Quel mé-
pris! il faut plier à ces formats le grand Homme-Volant. Que de
fois je l'ai vu, du Peyrou, traverser, de la mer à l'Occident, crever
les cercles du ciel fin. Il faisait ses expériences—dans l'air, sur sa
machine devenue inséparable—mais en réalité sur *moi*. Était-ce
apprendre à lire? Quel alphabet!"[13] In the very text of the letter,
while complaining about the drudgery of the assignment, the poet,
inspired by another ideal figure, creates a magnificent metaphor:
Leonardo, the inventor who promised man the sky, a modern Dae-
dalus, writing his indelible signs into the heaven and the hearts of
posterity.

This "commande" has become, like the "Teste" fragments, one
of Valéry's most celebrated texts; in 1919 it was republished in
La Nouvelle Revue Française, preceded by "Note et digression," and
these were again republished in 1933, along with a third essay,
"Léonard et les Philosophes (Lettre à Ferrero)," which had first
appeared separately in *Commerce* in 1928. All three texts were now
accompanied by marginal notes, written between 1929 and 1933.
This annotated trilogy of texts, dating from 1894, 1919, and 1929
(*O*, I, 1154-1296), constitutes an integral part of Valéry's phenomen-
ology of artistic perception and aesthetics, and it celebrates not the
historical Italian artist and inventor, but rather a universal self which
reflects the poet's ideal.

Valéry was aware of this while writing *his* "Léonard"; in another
letter to Gide of February 1895, he relates: "Vinci est au plus mal!

---

[13] *Gide-Valéry, Correspondance,* p. 299.

Je l'ai montré à Drouin ... qui vers la treizième page m'a fait observer que je ne parlais pas de Vinci. Je ne le savais que trop. Mais que dire de cet être?" [14] And in one of the marginal notes, added to the original text many years later, the author explains: "en réalité, j'ai nommé *homme* et *Léonard* ce qui m'apparaissait alors comme le pouvoir de l'esprit" (*O*, I, 1155). The "que peut un homme?" is Leonardo's obsession as it was Teste's; and his motto is "*Hostinato rigore,*" which had been that of the historical Leonardo. Again, like Teste, Leonardo is the hero of "the Possible; " another marginal note reads: "...ma tentative fut plutôt de concevoir et de décrire à ma façon le *Possible d'un Léonard* que le Léonard de l'Histoire" (*O*, I, 1203-04). Leonardo is, like Teste, a hero of the "regard," the "regard d'Ange." A Notebook entry of the thirties reads: "Roman Conte Description par l'*ange*-Lionardo. L'ange - celui qui voit les divers ordres" (*Cahiers*, XVI, 841); the note then continues contrasting this angelic vision with the common, human one.

Leonardo, the artist, has that pure vision which Valéry celebrated in his early prose poem "Purs Drames" (*O*, I, 1597-99); in the "Introduction," he says that "la plupart des gens ... voient par l'intellect bien plus souvent que par les yeux," and a marginal note reads: "une œuvre d'art devrait toujours nous apprendre que nous n'avons pas vu ce que nous voyons" (*O*, I, 1165). This "innocent," angelic vision is uncontaminated by habit and convention, and Valéry discusses it frequently in his aesthetic notations: "il est de ma nature mentale de me trouver tout à coup *devant* les choses comme tout inconnues—et comme de mesurer du regard *toute* la distance entre elles et ce moi qui doit les subir ou accomplir, *sans le secours de l'habitude, des conventions, des moyens déjà connus* (*Cahiers*, XVI, 370). Or, "le 'penseur' est devant la 'pensée' comme l'artiste devant les choses sensibles; et il doit, comme lui, faire effort pour nettoyer son œil, et *voir* au lieu de lire" (*Cahiers*, XVIII, 401). Armed with this pure perception, Leonardo confronts the phenomenal world and masters it: "il est le maître des visages, des anatomies, des machines. Il sait de quoi se fait un sourire" (*O*, I, 1175). In a *Notebook* entry of the twenties, entitled, "Lionardo," Valéry says that Leonardo possesses, like no other artist, the precise sense of the forms

---

[14] Ibid., p. 232.

of nature and concludes: "il est l'ange de la morphologie" (*Cahiers,*
XI, 199). Leonardo's "regard pur" is, of course, Valéry's; another
entry of those years reads: "Ange. Entrangeté des choses (du soleil,
de la figure des hommes, etc.). Et c'est en quoi je suis 'Ange' "
(*Cahiers,* VIII, 880).

It is as an artist — "l'artiste du monde même" — that Leonardo
differs from Teste; for whereas the latter lives almost entirely in
and by his "esprit," Leonardo passionately explores the phenomenal
world:

> Cet homme, qui a disséqué dix cadavres pour suivre le tra-
> jet de quelques veines, songe: l'organisation de notre corps
> est une telle merveille que l'âme, quoique *chose divine,* ne
> se sépare qu'avec les plus grandes peines de ce corps qu'elle
> habitait. (*O,* I, 1213)

The most significant dogma of the Church for Leonardo, therefore,
is that of the resurrection of the body, because "rien de plus pauvre
que cette âme qui a perdu son corps." But while the body's marvelous design and beauty unceasingly preoccupy that master artist, its
ugliness does not escape him. For example, "la machine érotique
l'intéresse," and Leonardo's sketches of embracing lovers show their
"transformation en bêtes." "Ce regard assez froid sur la mécanique
de l'amour," Valéry notes marginally, "est unique, je crois, dans
l'histoire intellectuelle" (*O,* I, 1213).

Leonardo, like Teste, aspires to the angelic vision which reduces
the world to its object, without being itself object for another:

> C'est une manière de lumineux supplice que de sentir que
> l'on voit tout sans cesser de sentir que l'on est encore *visi-*
> *ble,* et l'objet concevable d'une attention étrangère; et sans
> se trouver jamais le poste ni le regard qui ne laissent rien
> derrière eux. (*O,* I, 1217)

This Angel's "luminous torture" simply is that he is not God! The
brightest of angels, Lucifer, who fell through pride, is celebrated
elsewhere in Valéry's poetry.

In subsequent passages of "Note et digression," Valéry analyzes "l'intelligence" of the *Moi* which now transcends the phenomenal and the temporal:

> Comme chaque *chose visible* est à la fois étrangère, indispensable, et inférieure à la *chose qui y voit,* ainsi l'importance de ces figures, si grande qu'elle apparaisse à chaque instant, pâlit à la réflexion devant la seule persistance de l'attention elle-même. Tout le cède à cette universalité pure, à cette généralité insurmontable que la conscience se sent être. (*O,* I, 1217-18)

The more perfect the system, the further is it removed from its (physiological) origins:

> ...un système complet de substitutions psychologiques, plus il est conscient et se remplace par lui-même, plus il se détache de toute origine, et plus se dépouille-t-il, en quelque sorte, de toute chance de rupture. Pareil à l'anneau de fumée, le système tout d'énergies intérieures prétend merveilleusement à une indépendance et à une insécabilité parfaites. (*O,* I, 1219)

Valéry is here discussing that *Moi pur* for which one of his favorite similes is the "Zéro mathématique," the figure for a state of being, totally neutral and without attribute, that has, however, limitless virtuality: substance without accident, potency without act. An entry of the forties explains both the concept and the image:

> La meilleure image du MOI est bien le Zéro, qui, d'une part, exprime le sans-attribut, ni image, ni valeur du "moi pur" qui s'obtient par exhaustion, puisque *tout* ce qui se propose à la conscience est un *Antégo* par là même; et d'autre part, le zéro multiplie par 10 le nombre donné ... lui communique une valeur aussitôt incomparable. ...Ainsi, ce *qui se connaît rien en soi* est cependant un excitant de *valeur incomparable.* (*Cahiers,* XXIV, 171)

In "Note et digression," he explains that "cette conscience accomplie...est donc différente du néant, d'aussi peu que l'on voudra," adding that "*l'homme de l'esprit* doit enfin se réduire sciemment à un refus indéfini d'être quoi que ce soit" (*O,* I, 1224, 1225). Like Teste's Leonardo-Valéry's *Moi pur* rejects its person(ality): "...la personnalité est composée de souvenirs, d'habitudes, de penchants, de réactions .... Or, tout ceci peut être regardé comme accidentel par rapport à la pure et simple conscience. Elle est au contraire parfaitement impersonnelle" (*O,* I, 1226-27).

Valéry's reasoning here is marked by a certain scholasticism, as is his notion of the Angel. In 1910, he had regularly attended the courses of Father P. Hurteaux on Saint Thomas Aquinas' *Summa* (cf. *O*, I, 34), and the Thomistic angels — those pure Intelligences, each one a species to itself — have left their mark on Valéry's. Leonardo-Valéry's marvelous intellect immolates the individual that possesses it, or is possessed by it, to become a unique and universal Self: "se sent conscience pure; il ne peut pas en exister deux. [Il] est le moi, le pronom universel, appelation de *ceci* qui n'a pas de rapport avec un visage" (*O*, I, 1229). "L'esprit," says Valéry elsewhere, "se trouve environné d'esprits; chacun est comme le centre d'un peuple de semblables, il est l'*unique,* et il n'est cependant que quelque unité de ce nombre indéterminé; *il est à la fois incomparable et quelconque*" ("La Politique de l'Esprit," *O*, I, 1029). In another essay, Valéry notes that

> ce que j'avais dit des triangles, saint Thomas le professe des Anges, lesquels étant tout immatériels et des essences séparées, chacun d'eux est nécessairement seul de son espèce. Il faudrait donc en toute rigueur ne jamais dire deux triangles, ni deux anges, mais un triangle et un triangle, un ange et un ange. (*O*, II, 955)

In the Leonardo da Vinci essays, Valéry has given us a personified image of his ideal and aspirations — "quant au vrai Léonard, il fut ce qu'il fut" (*O*, I, 1233).

CHAPTER IV

"L'ANGE FRAIS DE L'ŒIL NU," "LA JEUNE PARQUE," AND THE ANGELS OF *CHARMES*

When we turn to Valéry's lyric poetry of the period, the poems published in 1920 in *Album de vers anciens,* we realize that his "farewell to poetry" was indeed not absolute. Though many of the pieces of that *recueil* were written before the 1892 crisis, it contains several important poems written afterwards, though before "La Jeune Parque," whose composition spans the years 1913 to 1917. One of the most significant poems of the "période aiguë," the Teste years, [1] is "Profusion du soir" (O, I, 86-89). Valéry began the poem around 1899 and reworked it many times; it preoccupied him for about a quarter of a century, and its subtitle, "Poème abandonné...," certainly alludes to its creative history.

For Valéry no poem was ever "finished;" in "Mémoires du Poète" he explains that "une œuvre n'est jamais nécessairement *finie,* car celui qui l'a faite ne s'est jamais accompli" (O, I, 1450-51). He also liked to compare poetic to musical composition, in that poets could produce, "in the manner of musicians a diversity of variants and solutions of the same subject" (O, I, 1501). We have noted how this theory of composition is linked to the "fragmentary" form of much of the poet's work; [2] and it pertains eminently to "Profusion du soir," which is made up of fragments: one opening sonnet and

---

[1] Reminiscing, Valéry says: "je regrette le temps où je jouissais du souverain bien (cette liberté de l'esprit). ... Je ne souhaitais que le pouvoir du faire, et non son exercice dans le monde" (O, I, 1477).

[2] Cf. *Rhetoric.*

eleven "sections" of varying length and rhyme schemes, variations all on the "theme" of the abundance of a sunset.

Charles Whiting calls this poem Valéry's "premier grand poème de l'intellect;"[3] and James R. Lawler, in his thorough history and definitive exegesis of the poem, reminds us that it was important for Valéry to the very end of his creative career, as it is alluded to by the protagonist of *Mon Faust* of 1940.[4] For Lawler, "Profusion du soir" constitutes "a *contemplatio* in the literal sense of a solemn meditation on a sacred space, the confrontation of the eye with nature at its most bounteous."[5] For us, the poem is a hymn to the eye, the "regard d'Ange," and it introduces an image which integrates the Angel's purity with that of his vision: "L'Ange frais de l'œil nu." This "cool Angel of the naked eye" becomes the culmination of the opening sonnet's final tercet, and the eleven remaining fragments are all musical variations on the theme of the "regard." After the death of the sun, the "cool Angel of the naked eye" announces the birth of a thought in the mind and a star in the sky:

> L'Ange frais de l'œil nu pressent dans sa pudeur
> Haute nativité d'étoile élucidée,
> Un diamant agir qui berce la splendeur...

The poem's fragments are variations on the reciprocal interaction of world and mind through the eye that is fecundated by the phenomena of nature, out of which it creates the meaning which it confers on the world — "Une maternité muette de pensées."

These birth metaphors celebrate the fertile union of the male and the female, of the senses and the intellect, which underlies the entire "scene" of this "Théâtre pensif," the seascape — "Cette femme d'écume et d'algue et d'or que roule/Sur le sable et le sel la meule de la houle" — and the sky above it: "Pourtant je place aux cieux les ébats d'un esprit." In this sky, the eye forms divinities out of the clouds, and a swimming Angel whose every stroke measures the celestial space:

[3] Charles C. Whiting, *Valéry jeune poète* (Paris: Presses Universitaires de France, 1960), p. 123.

[4] James R. Lawler, *The Poet as Analyst* (Berkeley: University of California Press, 1974), pp. 74-116.

[5] *Ibid.*, p. 77.

> Et sur les roches d'air du soir qui s'assombrit,
> Telle divinité s'accoude. Un ange nage.
> Il restaure l'espace à chaque tour de rein.

The beautiful anagram itself marries the male and the female —
"ange" and "nage," the angel's union with the maternal *Urelement*.
The vision is, of course, entirely of the beholder's creation, his transformation of an evening cloud. The persona *is* an eye-protagonist,
who has shed the "person," so that the poem poetizes this process
so frequently described in the Notebooks, and in prose texts like
"Monsieur Teste" and "Note et digression":

> Moi, qui jette ici-bas l'ombre d'un personnage,
> Toutefois délié dans le plein souverain,
> Je me sens qui me trempe, et pur qui me dédaigne!

The shadow of the "personnage" is not merely "cast," but "thrown
off," and this self-disdain has rendered the *Moi pur*.

The eye was likewise the protagonist of Valéry's early prose
poem, "Purs Drames" (*O*, I, 1597-99),[6] whose title could also have
fittingly designated "Profusion du soir." It was published in 1892,
and again in 1931; and while "Profusion" celebrates a sunset, "Purs
Drames" is a poem about sunrise, about the *de-venir* of a world
apprehended by sight. "Un œil pur" is the protagonist of the drama
about to unfold: the poet's matutinal, angelic eye projects its "lueur
lustrale" upon phenomena in which it recognizes fragments of the
original unity of the universe. The eye of "Purs Drames" is a "celestial pool," whose fine mirror reflects the sky, while *thinking* its
images. Sight and insight together finally reduce a reminiscence of
Eden and the symbolic morning garden to the line of dawn rising
on the late night sky: "Aime donc le Drame pur d'une ligne sur
l'espace de couleur céleste ou vitale." Both the verse of "Profusion
du soir" and the prose of "Purs Drames" celebrate the pure vision
of "l'Ange frais de l'œil nu."

The publication of "La Jeune Parque" in 1917 marked Valéry's
triumphant "return" to poetry. The poem's subject is related to that
of "Agathe," as its creator explains: "le sujet véritable du poème

---

[6] We discussed the prose poem and its importance to Valéry elsewhere
(Chap. I, n. 5).

est la peinture d'une suite de substitutions psychologiques, et en somme le changement d'une conscience pendant la durée d'une nuit" (*O*, I, 1613). But now the "theme" is fully orchestrated. In a letter of the year in which the poem appeared, Valéry relates its theme to Poe's "Consciousness," and then proceeds to discuss this intellectual subject's lyric composition:

> le sujet vague de l'œuvre est la Conscience de soi-même; la Consciousness de Poe, si l'on veut.
> ...Faire un chant prolongé, sans action, rien que l'incohérence interne aux confins du sommeil; y mettre autant d'*intellectualité* que j'ai pu le faire et que la poésie en peut admettre sous ses voiles; sauver l'abstraction prochaine par la musique, ou la racheter par des visions, voilà ce que j'ai fini par me résoudre à essayer, et je ne l'ai pas toujours trouvé facile. ... Je n'ai pu me tirer de l'affaire qu'en travaillant par morceaux. [7]

"La Jeune Parque," then, constitutes another transformation of the great subtext — "la Conscience de soi-même" — now musically orchestrated into lyric fragments which the poet has likened to *recitativi* for contralto. And though the figure of the Angel is not manifest in the poem's "surface" imagery, the Ange/Narcisse configuration is an inherent part of its underlying "deep-structure":

> Harmonieuse MOI, différente d'un songe,
> Femme flexible et ferme aux silences suivis
> D'actes purs! ...
> . . . .
> Dites! ...j'étais l'égale et l'épouse du jour,
> Seul support souriant que je formais d'amour
> A la toute-puissante altitude adorée... (*O*, I, 99)

The harmoniousness of this *moi* recalls the Angel, as do the "pure acts" and the upward surge of love to the sun, whose support is the adoring mind. "Altitude adorée" constitutes a wordplay in suggesting "altitude dorée," "golden altitude," the sun. As she envisions her death, the Young Fate mourns that of the universe, for her mind carries its meaning, is its mirror and reflection:

---

[7] Valéry, *Lettres à quelques-uns*, pp. 124-25.

> Tout l'univers chancelle et tremble sur ma tige,
> La pensive couronne échappe à mes esprits. (O, I, 102)

The Fate's "crown of thought" recalls the Angel's "spiritual diadem," that "système étincelant comme un diadème." But at the end of her dramatic night, the Young Fate rejects the angelic "pureté du Non-être" for life. And after the poem's denouement, its *solemnitas* celebrates the marriage of *corps* and esprit, φ and ψ, in the world. Valéry consistently designates this union by the sign of "C E M" in the Notebooks: "C E M—le mon-corps, le mon-esprit, le mon-monde ce sont 3 directions—qui se dessinent toujours—et 3 domaines" (*Cahiers*, XXV, 710). The entry is from 1942; Valéry's great poem had orchestrated the drama of "C E M" twenty-five years earlier.

Valéry told us how, after the years of patient and passionate work on his major poem, the "Charmes" burst forth almost spontaneously, so that the poem which had originally been planned as a farewell came to mark his return to poetry. The opening and the concluding poems of *Charmes*, "Aurore" and "Palme," were written immediately after completion of "La Jeune Parque":

> Ce poème achevé, j'ai fait presque aussitôt, et d'abondance, *Aurore* et *Palme*, comme si la raideur et la longueur de mon effort étaient récompensées par une légèreté et une aisance qui ne peuvent succéder qu'à quelque entraînement rigoureux et volontaire. (O, I, 1613)

Not inspiration, but mastery of a technique acquired over nearly four years of assiduous application, makes the master poet. Elsewhere Valéry, reflecting on the influence of Poe, risks "shocking" the popular notion about poetic inspiration by confessing: "j'aimerais mieux avoir composé une œuvre médiocre en toute lucidité qu'un chef-d'œuvre à éclairs dans un état de transe" (O, I, 1481). Ironically, the poet of the masterpieces probably never fully realized that his predecessor had, indeed, lucidly composed some mediocre poems! At any rate, after the composition of "La Jeune Parque," the two poems that here concern us came to Valéry virtually without effort, almost like a reward for his hard work:

> alors, ayant achevé ma *Jeune Parque*, il m'est arrivé quelques semaines après, d'écrire en très peu de temps, très

> rapidement, *Aurore* et *Palme,* et j'ai eu l'impression moi-
> même qu'ayant fait de l'escrime avec une barre de plomb
> j'en faisais avec un fleuret. Je me sentais en possession
> d'une liberté durement acquise dans le métier de faire des
> vers... (*O,* I, 1614)

Originally, moreover, "Aurore" and "Palme" were the same poem, and their kinship is still recognizable in their common stanzaic form as well as a certain parallelism of the vocabulary, which has been examined by Lawler.[8] In a previous study we discussed at some length the importance of the theme of dawn in Valéry's prose poetry. Dawn is preeminently the moment of the *Moi pur,* and "Aurore" (*O,* I, 111-13) is its lyric celebration. Like many of the prose aubades, "Aurore" is introspective in singing the awakening of a "paysage d'âme" rather than that of an objective matutinal landscape. It celebrates the awakening of the poetic consciousness. The poet greets the harmonious syllables of the song forming in his mind, imaged in the most sensuous vocabulary: his matutinal enthusiasm mounts the quivering rungs of a golden ladder, from which he beholds groups of words come to life like women awakening in the morning sun, objects of his desire. Their voluptuous beauty has seduced the poetic *moi,* and under their spell he rejects Thought for Delight, breaking the "spiritual net" of his thoughts to explore the "oracle of his sensuous forest":

> Leur toile spirituelle
> Je la brise, et vais cherchant
> Dans ma forêt sensuelle
> Les oracles de mon chant.

Then the introspective poem, poetizing the poet-persona's consciousness at dawn, his "esprit," sings a morning hymn to desire and the beauty of the emerging world. *Corps* and *esprit* come together in an act of love, whose virile eroticism assures both self-possession and possession of the world:

> Il n'est pour ravir un monde
> De blessure si profonde
> Qui ne soit au ravisseur

---

[8] James R. Lawler, *Lecture de Valéry* (Paris: Presses Universitaires de France, 1963), p. 31.

> Une féconde blessure,
> Et son propre sang l'assure
> D'être le vrai possesseur.

In the poem's denouement, Hope is imaged as the beautiful swimmer in a transparent, invisible pool; she is the feminine complement to the Angel swimming in the evening clouds of "Profusion du soir":

> Son col coupe le temps vague
> Et soulève cette vague
> Que fait un col sans pareil...
> Elle sent sous l'onde
> La profondeur infinie,
> Et frémit depuis l'orteil.

While "Aurore" celebrates the poet's morning confidence, and his virile taking possession of the world, "Palme" (O, I, 153-56), again about the creative process, appears to be the other poem's feminine counterpart. It is indeed its "other half," a poem about maternity: in the form of a parable, it tells of the secret gestation and patient maturation, finally the miraculous birth of the poem — the palm tree's "fruit mûr." The tree is one of Valéry's richest symbols for the mind, its roots (φ) anchored deep in the maternal earth, and its crown (ψ) reaching toward the sun. [9]

Both the symbol of the Palm and the form of the parable confer a Biblical tonality on the poem, whose religious solemnity is enhanced by the appearance of an Angel "of formidable grace" in the opening stanza. It is the Angel of the Annunciation who visits the poet to bring him his gifts of both earthly and spiritual foods, and who "speaks to his vision":

> De sa grâce redoutable
> Voilant à peine l'éclat,
> Un ange met sur ma table
> Le pain tendre, le lait plat;
> Il me fait de la paupière
> Le signe d'une prière
> Qui parle à ma vision:

---

[9] Cf. Pierre Laurette, *Le Thème de l'arbre chez Valéry* (Paris: Klincksieck, 1967).

—Calme, calme, reste calme!
Connais le poids d'une palme
Portant sa profusion!

This is the loveliest Angel in Valéry's lyric poetry. A *Notebook* entry from his later years reads:

> Les Ecritures sont pleines de thèmes extraordinairement beaux. Plus riches que les anciens - lesquels ont trop de mythes à monstres. L'Annonciation est une merveille - Bien Léonardesque - avec l'émoi et le mystère de la Fécondation - en dessous. Le point de tendresse critique situé entre l'acte (ici, *mystique*) et le germe dans la chair de la vierge - C'est une idée extraordinaire, d'une "poésie" suprême - L'Ange l'annonce bien simplement, et il a grandement raison. (*Cahiers*, XXVI, 282)

Already, more than twenty years earlier, the poet had created the "Leonardesque beauty" and the "supreme poetry" of the Angel of the Annunciation in "Palme." "Scarcely veiling the glory of his formidable grace," the Angel of "Palme" has the stately simplicity of the Biblical one; his maternal gifts of tender bread and the — untranslatable — "lait plat" set the tone of this most tender of Valéry's poems. Like "Profusion du soir," it ends in a giving that is a receiving, that "haute maternité" of the creative act; the Angel announces:

Tu n'as pas perdu ces heures
Si légère tu demeures
Après ces beaux abandons;
Pareille à celui qui pense
Et dont l'âme se dépense
A s'accroître de ses dons!

The best-known of the "Charmes" is Valéry's great elegiac meditation, "Le Cimetière marin" (*O,* I, 147-51), first published in 1920, with a different strophic arrangement than that of the final version, and without the Pindaric epigraph. There is no better succinct commentary on the poem's *forme* and *fond* than the poet's own. In 1933, the poet explained both the genesis and the intent of his famous poem in "Au Sujet du *Cimetière marin*" (*O,* I, 1496-1507), how it first imposed itself on the poetic consciousness as a rhythm, then a metric and strophic figure that needed to be "filled: "

Quant au *Cimetière marin,* cette intention ne fut d'abord
qu'une figure rythmique vide .... Il me proposa une certaine strophe de six vers et l'idée d'une *composition* fondée sur le nombre de ces strophes, et assurée par une diver-
sité de tons et de fonctions à leur assigner. Entre les
strophes, des contrastes ou des correspondances devaient
être institués. Cette dernière condition exigea bientôt que
le poème possible fût un monologue de "moi," dans lequel
les thèmes les plus simples et les plus constants de ma vie
affective et intellectuelle, tels qu'ils s'étaient imposés à mon
adolescence et associés à la mer et à la lumière d'un certain
lieu des bords de la Méditerranée, fussent appelés, tramés,
opposés...
   Tout ceci menait à la mort et touchait à la pensée.
...Je savais que je m'orientais vers un monologue aussi personnel, mais aussi universel que je pourrais le construire.
...Un assez long travail s'ensuivit. (*O,* I, 1503-4)

This recollection by the poet about the creative process of his most
dualistic poem itself constitutes the demonstration of that dualism:
it is one of the rare texts by a modern poet about poetry that dis-
sociates content and form. The form came first, then needed to be
filled. The themes to fill that form were to be from the poet's affective and his intellectual life, associated with sea and light, to culminate in the contrast of "la mort" and "la pensée pure." We find
here, again, the division between the angelic and the human, the
male — "lumière" — and the female — "water."

The poem's protagonist is, in fact, once more the *Moi* divided,
intellect and affect, ψ and φ, *corps* and *esprit,* in a *monde* of sun
and sea, a setting structured out of the poet's personal memories
which, at the same time, celebrates the universal, archetypal, elements
of fire and water, symbols of "esprit" and "corps." The lucid Self
is alone, high up in the sun-drenched cemetery overlooking the sea,
with the countless Dead "sleeping" below in the dark, his mind
aspiring to transcend the body that partakes of the universal mutability. This, as we noted, is one of Valéry's most dualistic poems,
where the antithetical motifs of "ombre" and "lumière," the transcending "pensée pure" and decomposition, timelessness and cyclical
return, life and death, the universal and the personal, are contrapuntally invoked, interwoven, and set in opposition. Valéry said,
"j'ai écrit une 'partition' " (*O,* I, 1506); it is the score of a fugue

whose themes are the contrasting "moments de ce *moi*," its angelic aspiration and its human limitation.

From his high vantage point — "A ce point pur je monte et m'accoutume,/Tout entouré de mon regard marin" — the persona beholds a world reflecting the *Moi pur:* a many-faceted diamond, created by the marriage of sun and sea:

> Quel pur travail de fins éclairs consume
> Maint diamant d'imperceptible écume,
> Et quelle paix semble se concevoir!
> Quand sur l'abîme un soleil se repose,
> Ouvrages purs d'une éternelle cause,
> Le Temps scintille et le Songe est savoir.

As the "pure toil" and "pure creations" of the elements "consume" the particular, as the "imperceptible foam" over the abyss is absorbed in the universal luminosity, and Time becomes a "flicker" against eternity, so in the mind, too, all particular thoughts are consumed by the luminous object of its contemplation, which *is* its knowledge. The person(al) has disappeared, and the *moi* and its world are pure luminosity. We recall a *Notebook* entry of the poet's later years, in which he remarks that angels are made of all-consuming fire, "...la *Nature Angélique*—Qu'entends-tu par ces mots? Ce qui est *pur en soi*—qui touche à tout, et n'est par rien touché . . . . ce qui refuse d'avoir été — ce qui veut tout consumer—Ignis sunt. 'L'acte pur' des scholastiques" (*Cahiers*, XXI, 596).

The following stanza spells out the analogy of the object of vision with the mind that beholds it, as the sunlit sea becomes a temple of wisdom and the vast eye of the mind:

> Stable trésor, temple simple à Minerve,
> . . . .
> Eau sourcilleuse, Oeil qui gardes en toi
> Tant de sommeil sous un voile de flamme,
> O mon silence! ...Edifice dans l'âme.

The external is internalized, the internal externalized: the world is reflected and mirrored in a mind that in return gives it its meaning. But after the *moment privilégié* of this perfect marriage, the *Moi angélique* abdicates his hybris in an apostrophe to the sky, and now

assumes his (human) mutability and mortality, not without once more
recalling his (angelic) pride and power:

> Beau ciel, vrai ciel, regarde-moi qui change!
> Après tant d'orgueil, après tant d'étrange
> Oisiveté, mais pleine de pouvoir,
> Je m'abandonne à ce brillant espace,
> Sur les maisons des morts mon ombre passe
> Qui m'apprivoise à son frêle mouvoir.

His "shadow" passing over the graves is the sign of the *Moi*'s
mortality; and that shadow also suggests the passing of the sun
beyond the high point of noon, that illusory instant of the meridian
when Time appears to stand still for a fragment of eternity.

Though the definitive version of the poem contains no angel,
except those sculptures vainly decorating the graves — "Éloignez-en
les prudentes colombes,/Les songes vains, les anges curieux" — the
Moi's "orgueil" and the hybris projecting the self beyond the human
condition are traits of the Valéryan *Moi angélique* par excellence.
In examining early drafts of the poem, Lloyd J. Austin has discovered a version of the above stanza containing a "great angel" in the
first line:

> Grand ciel, beau ciel, éclat du temps, grand ange,
> Après tant d'amour, après tant d'étrange
> Oisiveté, mais pleine de pouvoir
> Je te regarde admirable justice
> L'âme exposée aux torches du solstice
> Marche son rêve au son pur du devoir. [10]

The second half of this stanza has in the definitive form been
incorporated into the first part of the following one, the fragments
thus being re-arranged:

> L'âme exposée aux torches du solstice,
> Je te soutiens, admirable justice
> De la lumière aux armes sans pitié!
> Je te rends pure à ta place première:
> Regarde-toi!...Mais rendre la lumière
> Suppose d'ombre une morne moitié.

---

[10] Lloyd J. Austin, "Paul Valéry compose *Le Cimetière marin*" in *Mercure
de France* (janvier-avril 1953), p. 600.

Here the *Moi* has become the mirror of the universe, its pure consciousness and conscience: "Tout l'univers chancelle et tremble sur ma tige," said the Young Fate. But like the mirror, and like the sea, the mind has a dark underside, without which it could not reflect the light.

After contemplating the graveyard and its white marble tombs trembling in the noon heat, after glancing down to the sea below, which by a visual illusion appears like a "tranquil roof" over the graves — "La mer fidèle y dort sur mes tombeaux" — the protagonist raises his mind's eye once more up to the fire which would blind his mortal vision:

> Midi là-haut, Midi sans mouvement
> En soi se pense et convient à soi-même...
> Tête complète et parfait diadème,
> Je suis en toi le secret changement.

Here, at the pivotal moment of the poem, the *Moi* confronts the Absolute, an unmoved, self-sufficient, mover of the universe — that exists, however, only in the mind which anthropomorphizes the divinities it creates, a mind whose mortal body already throws a secret shadow, as the sun begins to decline. The self-sufficient and self-thinking solar "tête complète et parfait diadème" recalls "Agathe's" independent spiritual system, "le système étincelant comme un diadème" of the Angel, as well as his "couronne de la connaissance unitive."

One year after "Le Cimetière marin," Valéry published "Ébauche d'un Serpent" (*O,* I, 138-46) on which he had been working for several years. One of his longest poems, it retells the third Chapter of *Genesis,* the temptation and fall of Eve. But the poem's protagonist is the tempter, of whom the Bible says: "Now the serpent was more subtil than any beast of the field which the Lord God had made" (Genesis, III, 1). And Valéry's subtle serpent does not fail to remind us that he was the brightest of the Angels before his Fall, Lucifer, the "Lightbearer" and Morning star.

Valéry's fascination with the serpent — he chose a serpent entwined around a key as his personal emblem — and especially with the archetypal uroboros, the serpent swallowing its tail (sketches of which abound in the *Notebooks*), lies beyond the scope of our discussion. What concerns us here is the serpent's angelic past that has made him what he is in the Garden: the devil, who never forgets his former proximity to the divine, whose ways he therefore knows better than any other creature.

We have noted that the motif of the Fall is inseparable from Valéry's Angel figure, and not merely from his early Angel — "chu de l'azur facile aux portes de la tombe" — but that the notion of the Fall is also intrinsically related to the mature "angelic self," whose construction is inspired by an aspiration to a "higher" state. Among the numerous *Notebook* passages on the Fall which have found their way into Valéry's published work are two fragments from *Tel quel* (*O,* II, 696), which have a direct bearing on our poem:

> L'Ange ne diffère du démon que par une certaine réflexion qui ne s'est point encore présentée à lui.
> *Chutes*
> a) Il y a eu deux grandes et mystérieuses chutes. Chute des Anges, chute de l'homme: catastrophes *homothétiques,* dirait un géomètre.
> *Tout ce qu'IL fit devait donc tomber:*
> b) Toute religion fondée sur l'idée d'une *chute* initiale se trouve en proie aux douleurs de la discontinuité.
> c) Mais une Création est une première rupture. A l'origine du monde deux actes, l'un du créateur, l'autre de la créature, l'un fonde la foi, et l'autre...la liberté.

With "homothetic," i.e., "similar in construction and position," Valéry points to a parallelism not merely between the Fall of the Angels and the Fall of Man — but between the Fall of Man and the Fall of God! For God's Fall, as the poem's Serpent will explain, is the very Creation itself: "une Création est une première rupture." Thus logically, "Tout ce qu'IL fit devait donc tomber"! The entire universe is a "flaw" in the primal pure Nothingness. The Serpent, fallen Morningstar, apostrophizes the Sun, in which he salutes not the "perfect diadem" of the "Cimetière marin," but "his proudest accomplice" in deception, the "glaring Error" masking Death:

> Soleil, soleil! ...Faute éclatante!
> Toi qui masques la mort, Soleil,
> Sous l'azur et l'or d'une tente
> Où les fleurs tiennent leur conseil;

Par d'impénétrables délices,
Toi, le plus fier de mes complices,
Et de mes pièges le plus haut,
Tu gardes les cœurs de connaître
Que l'univers n'est qu'un défaut
Dans la pureté du Non-être!

Nor was the "Cimetière's" protagonist deceived when he said:

Et vous, grande âme, espérez-vous un songe
Qui n'aura plus ces couleurs de mensonge
Qu'aux yeux de chair l'onde et l'or font ici?

(O, I, 150)

The sun is a flaming "king of shadows," for it calls into being a
world condemned to death:

Grand Soleil, qui sonnes l'éveil
A l'être, et de feux l'accompagnes,
. . . .
Trompeusement peint de campagnes
Fauteur des fantômes joyeux
. . . .
Toujours le mensonge m'a plu
Que tu répands sur l'absolu,
O roi des ombres fait de flamme!

Teste, the angelic and the pure — "dur comme un ange" — had,
we recall, disdained to manifest his essence, for the Fault and Fall
of genius is to make itself known. Teste had preferred himself: "Je
me suis préféré. Ce qu'ils nomment un être supérieur est un être
qui s'est trompé" (O, II, 15). From the "être supérieur" to the
"Highest" it is but a step. "Chaque esprit qu'on trouve puissant,
commence par la faute qui le fait connaître" (O, II, 16); and "le
Tout-puissant" is no exception! But listen to the Serpent:

Cieux, son erreur! Temps, sa ruine!
Et l'abîme animal, béant!...
Quelle chute dans l'origine
Étincelle au lieu de néant!...
Mais, le premier mot de son Verbe,
MOI!...Des astres le plus superbe
Qu'ait parlés le fou créateur,

Je suis!...Je serai!...J'illumine
La diminution divine
De tous les feux du Séducteur!

Is God, then, more "human" than Teste?

Valéry's Lucifer, his Serpent in the Garden, is not merely Biblical, but also poetic; nowhere else does the Devil sing such an
apostrophe to Light. Thus he will succeed, of course, in seducing
"l'Eve suave" with "ce plus rare des arts," for "of gauze there is
none so fine," nothing so delicate and sure, "Ni de fil invisible et
sûr,/Plus qu'une trame de mon style!" The Fallen Angel and Seducer
is a Poet!

Toward the end of his life, reflecting on the work he has created
and on that which he has left undone, Valéry muses: "Age, dégra-
dation... c'est que je me trouve par-ci par-là en présence du seigneur
Yo-Mismo—Non de ce 'moi pur', mon éternel agent—Mais d'un
personnage *Moi*—Auteur de telles œuvres... Je découvre que j'ai fait
—tout autres choses que celles que je pensais avoir faites. Je me dis,
avec mon Serpent que l'être est un défaut dans la pureté du Non-
être" (*Cahiers*, XXVIII, 89 [1944]).

CHAPTER V

THE ANGEL'S DEFEAT AND THE DIALOGUES

With the major poems of *Charmes,* Valéry's poetic career reaches its zenith, and this period of creative fecundity coincides with the second of the "deux événements formidables de ma vie secrète," the encounter with "Béatrice" (Catherine Pozzi). The angelic self is threatened by a great human love that will leave indelible marks. While the youthful crisis of the 90s had been exorcised by "Monsieur Teste," Béatrice will "chastise" his creator for the idolatry which accomplished that exorcism — "je confesse que j'ai fait une Idole de mon esprit, mais je n'en ai pas trouvé d'autre" (*O,* II, 37). A contemporary *Notebook* entry reads: "O Lionardo [Béatrice's appelation for the poet] che tanto pensate! Amour fut la récompense et le châtiment tout inattendue de cette quantité de pensées" (*Cahiers,* VIII, 374). And from the same *Notebook,* alluding to Dante's vision of the Dark Forest at the opening of *Inferno* i, "Béatrice—In mezzo del cammin—Las, blasé des choses de l'esprit— Limite. Trouve enfer et paradis—Mais qu'est-ce que les choses de l'esprit?" (*Cahiers,* VIII, 751). And as regards Monsieur Teste, "Love and Mr. Teste—Il fait sa théorie et puis—*Jamais en paix*" (*Cahiers,* X, 538, 531).

As the early crisis was instrumental in the construction of the angelic self, so the mature one marked its evolution as reflected in the mirror of the œuvre; this is always the basic justification for any critic's concern with the biographical notations of a writer's journal. Valéry himself, many years later, points to the importance of these experiences in their effect on the *Ego scriptor:*

Août 40 Insomnie...je revis ma grande maladie mentale d'amour de 91-92—et quelques années après—...La littérature ou plutôt, tout ce qui est spirituel, fut toujours mon anti-vie, mon anesthésique. Mais ces sensations cependant furent un puissant excitant intellectuel—le mal exaspérait le remède—*Eupalinos* en 21, *La Danse* en 22, écrits en état de ravage. Et qui le devinerait? (*Cahiers*, XXIII, 589-90)

"Eupalinos ou l'architecte" and "L'Ame et la danse," both of 1921, distinguish Valéry as the master of yet another form of poetic expression, the Socratic Dialogue. Both were written "sur commande," and in a letter of the thirties about the genesis of "Eupalinos," the poet explains to what extent the "order" imposed the form.[1] About the form of "L'Ame et la danse," Valéry writes: "Quant à la forme d'ensemble, j'ai tenté de faire du *Dialogue* lui-même une manière de ballet dont l'Image et l'Idée sont tour à tour les Coryphées. L'abstrait et le sensible mènent tour à tour et s'unissent enfin dans le vertige;" and in the same letter he adds:

je n'aurais jamais projeté d'écrire sur la danse, à laquelle je n'avais jamais sérieusement pensé. D'ailleurs j'estimais,—et je l'estime encore,—que Mallarmé avait épuisé le sujet en tant qu'il appartient à la littérature. Cette conviction m'a fait d'abord refuser la commande de la *Revue musicale*. D'autres raisons m'ont déterminé à l'accepter. Ce que Mallarmé avait prodigieusement écrit est alors devenu une condition singulière de mon travail.[2]

In both Dialogues, we feel the influence of Valéry's Béatrice. "Eupalinos" (*O*, II, 77-147) is a Dialogue of the Dead, in which the shades of Phèdre and Socrates, now free of the bonds of space and time, nostalgically recall their mortal existence. They evoke

[1] Valéry, *Lettres à quelques-uns*, p. 214: "...la commande déterminait le nombre de lettres que l'écrivain devait donner à composer: 115.800 *signes*. Cette rigueur, d'abord étonnante et rebutante, mais exigée d'un homme assez accoutumé à celle des poèmes à forme fixe, l'a fait songer d'abord; trouver ensuite que la forme singulière à lui proposée pouvait être assez aisément satisfaite en employant la forme très élastique du *Dialogue*."
[2] Ibid., pp. 190-91. We previously discussed the treatment of the theme in Mallarmé, Valéry, and Rilke. Cf. "Mallarmé's Living Metaphor: Valéry's Athikté and Rilke's 'Spanish Dancer'," in *Pre-Text, Text, Context: Essays in Nineteenth-Century French Literature* (Columbus: Ohio State University Press, 1980), pp. 217-27.

figures of the past, like Phèdre's great architect friend, Eupalinos, and they quote lines by Mallarmé, "le très admirable Stephanos, qui parut tant de siècles après nous" (*O,* II, 88). Eupalinos is not among the dead, but his is a "living" presence, recalled by Phèdre's memories. That great builder had constructed temples inspired by love, and had thus metamorphosed life — and love — into art:

> Écoute, Phèdre (me disait-il encore), ce petit temple que j'ai bâti pour Hermès, ...—c'est peu de chose; quatre colonnes, un style très simple,—j'ai mis les souvenir d'un clair jour de ma vie. O douce métamorphose! Ce temple délicat, nul ne le sait, est l'image mathématique d'une fille de Corinthe, que j'ai heureusement aimée. ...Il vit pour moi! Il me rend ce que je lui ai donné...

Finally, Eupalinos' great apostrophe to his body becomes the poet-artist's prayer, a prose poem to his mortal form:

> O mon corps, qui me rappelez à tout moment ce tempérament de mes tendances, cet équilibre de mes organes, ces justes proportions de vos parties...prenez garde à mon ouvrage; enseignez-moi sourdement les exigences de la nature, et me communiquez ce grand art dont vous êtes doué... Donnez-moi de trouver dans votre alliance le sentiment des choses vraies; modérez, renforcez, assurez mes pensées...
>
> Mais ce corps et cet esprit, mais cette présence invinciblement actuelle, et cette absence créatrice qui se disputent l'être, et qu'il faut enfin composer; mais ce fini et cet infini que nous apportons, chacun selon sa nature, il faut à présent qu'ils s'unissent dans une construction bien ordonnée.

"Quelle prière sans exemple! " exclaims Socrates. Eupalinos' example "converts" Socrates, who in the "immense leisure" of immortality judges and condemns his mortal past and dreams of another life. "Qu'est-ce donc que tu veux peindre sur le néant?" asks Phèdre; and Socrates replies: "L'Anti-Socrate. ...Ce sera donc...le constructeur." Thus, as Alexandre Lazaridès concludes in his analysis of this Dialogue, "aveugle au monde et au corps, Socrate représente, dans le récit paradoxalement central d'*Eupalinos,* l'échec de l'esprit qui prétend à la suprématie par la voie de la connaissance, alors qu'il n'est là que pour mettre en relation le monde et le corps, et que, sans eux, il ne peut être." [3] Is it not, at the same time, "l'échec de l'ange," the chastisement of the *Moi pur*?

"L'Ame et la danse" (*O,* II, 148-76), as its very title suggests, celebrates both body and soul, as Socrates, his physician, Éryximaque, and Phèdre, at a banquet, discourse on the most bodily of the arts. While watching the performers, and above all, "Athikté la palpitante," Socrates' "midwifery" tries to bring forth an answer to his query: "O mes amis, qu'est-ce véritablement que la danse?"

In the letter from which we quoted above, Valéry explains that "la pensée constante du *Dialogue* est physiologique,—depuis les troubles digestifs du début prélude, jusqu'à syncope finale." The "physiological" is also accentuated, of course, by the fact that Socrates' principal interlocutor is Éryximaque, his physician, and that the three friends are banqueting as they discourse on art. At the very "début prélude," ironically, the physician asks the thinker for a "spiritual" remedy for overeating: "O Socrate," Éryximaque exclaims, "je meurs!... Donne-moi de l'esprit! Verse l'idée!... Porte à mon nez tes énigmes aiguës!... Mon âme n'est plus qu'un songe que fait la matière en lutte avec elle-même!" But Socrates offers the idea that "l'homme qui mange est le plus juste des hommes..."

But what is dance? Éryximaque, the physician—both Socrates' and Athikté's—considers it a beautiful body's perfect exercise: "et la belle fibre de son corps net et musculeux, de la nuque jusqu'au talon, se prononce et se tord progressivement; et le tout frémit." For Phèdre, dance is mimetic, and Athikté "représente quelque chose." He insists: "Socrate, toute, elle était l'amour!...Mais regardez-la, n'est-elle pas soudain une véritable vague de la mer? ...C'est l'onde!" Socrates, finally, according to his celebrated "method," proves them both wrong and both right, and brings forth a new synthesis: the dancer represents "nulle chose, cher Phèdre. Mais toute chose, Éryximaque. Aussi bien l'amour comme la mer, et la vie elle-même, et les pensées... Ne sentez-vous pas qu'elle est l'acte pur des métamorphoses?" Beholding Athikté dance, Socrates feels himself "invaded by extraordinary forces;" her dance is a "festival of the body" offering light and joy to the soul: "cette fête du corps devant nos âmes offre lumière et joie..."

---

[3] Alexandre Lazaridès, *Valéry pour une Poétique du Dialogue* (Montréal: Presses de l'Université de Montréal, 1978), p. 176.

Both "esprit" and "corps," as Valéry's Leonardo had taught earlier, inspire every artist and creator. And, inspired by his Béatrice, the poet celebrates the body and its arts which enlighten the soul and mind. "Si *L'Ame et la danse*," comments Lazaridès, "constitue la réussite suprême des dialogues, c'est parce que les corps y parlent par la danse, et que la parole y prend corps par la poésie; les deux plans y sont donc constamment fondus." [4]

Eupalinos' temple was a "douce métamorphose" of love, and Athikté's dance is "l'acte pur des métamorphoses"; in the "Cimetière marin," the sun had transformed the sea below by its "pur travail," and the poem's persona saw in this marriage of the life-giving elements the "ouvrages purs" of an "eternal cause," that, from time immemorial, man has called God. God, according to the Scholastics, whom Valéry knew well, is Pure Act; but in this poetic universe that has no transcendent god, the notion of the Pure Act is associated with the angelic: "la Nature Angélique... ce qui est *pur en soi*—qui touche à tout, et n'est par rien touché...'L'acte pur' des scholastiques" (*Cahiers*, XXI, 596).

It will be recalled that Valéry had already, before the "Béatrice" crisis, become an "Anti-Teste," namely the creative poet whose conversion is reflected in the "Anti-Socrate" sketched out by Socrates himself in the Dialogue. Notebook entries of the early twenties mirror that change: "vers ce temps-là les hommes commencèrent à comprendre que la véritable connaissance est création... que la création est vie, que le faire est le seul savoir..." (*Cahiers*, VIII, 879). And a Leonardesque preoccupation with the body manifests itself frequently in the same *Notebook,* another of whose entries reads:

> le corps me semble la chose à étudier de près. Car il est lié à tout, et dans chaque événement φ ou ψ, ses parties ont des *valeurs* déterminées — Il est l'unique, le vrai, l'éternel, le complet, l'insurmontable, système de références. Mais comment ne le savons-nous pas toujours? Comment distinguons-nous cette 'connaissance' qui le *cache*? Tandis que d'autre part, le corps n'est que l'une des *choses* qu'elle contient, qu'elle définit? Qu'est donc cette connaissance? (*Cahiers*, VIII, 752)

---

[4] Ibid., p. 127.

And in one of the "Petites Études" of *Mélange,* Valéry remarks:

> l'esprit est à la merci du corps comme sont les aveugles à la
> merci des voyants qui les assistent. Le corps touche et fait
> tout; commence et achève tout. De lui émanent nos vraies
> lumières, et même les seules, qui sont nos besoins et nos
> appétits, par lesquels nous ayons une sorte de perception
> 'à distance' et superficielle de l'état de notre intime struc-
> ture. (*O,* I, 345)

A beautiful sequence of prose poems, entitled "A B C," written
in the early 20s, celebrates the marriage of "esprit" and "corps" to
form an undivided self which then salutes the world emerging at
dawn. We owe these texts again to a "commande," a literary "Alphabet" Valéry had been asked to write, but which was only
published in its full form in 1976.[5] The *Alphabet's* first three pieces,
the sequence "A B C," appeared separately in 1925,[6] and a modified
version of "A" was published in *Morceaux choisis* in 1930.

These texts, an interrelated unit among Valéry's many prose
aubades, constitute a series of three brief dramas, each one complete
and centered on the opposing forces of its inner tension, but all
sequentially related in the progressive development of a single theme:
the birth of the self and its world at dawn.[7] In "A" the mind finds
its body upon awakening at daybreak; in "B" mind and body unite
as the self arises to the new day; and in "C" the united self takes
possession of the world. As upon the awakening of consciousness
the self separates itself from the universal manifold and the *Moi*
emerges from the world — which it at the same time posits — that
self becomes divided into body and mind. Thus the three basic
Valéryan "points cardinaux de connaissance" upon which reality is
founded, and which he designates, as we noted above, by the sign
"C E M" in the Notebooks, constitute themselves.

In "A" the awakening mind — "mon esprit" — contemplates its
still sleeping body — "mon corps" — which has carried it through
the archetypal waters of night and unconsciousness like an ark, and
which preserves it:

---

[5] Paul Valéry, *Alphabet* (Paris: Blaizot, 1976).

[6] In *Commerce: Cahiers trimestriels,* 5 (automne 1925), 4-14.

[7] I discussed these texts in "A Valéryan Trilogy: The Prose Poems
'A B C'," in *The Centennial Review,* 20, 3, 244-56.

> ...arche close de vie qui transportes vers le jour mon his-
> toire et mes chances...tu es ma permanence inexprimable;
> ...ô ma forme fermée, je laisse toute pensée pour te con-
> templer de tout mon coeur.

This apostrophe recalls Eupalinos' morning "oraison" to his body's
perfect form. Like Narcissus leaning over the image which he loves,
our mind-persona embraces the form which gives him life and sus-
tains him: "Je me penche sur toi qui es moi;" and the waking lover
of this aubade sings to his sleeping beloved who holds him enchained:

> Il n'est pas de plus étrange, de plus pieuse pensée; il n'est
> pas de merveille plus proche. Mon amour devant toi est
> inépuisable... Tu m'attends sans me connaître et je te fais
> défaut pour me désirer.

Nowhere is Valéry's love poetry more passionate than in this morning song of the angelic male spirit, of animus to anima:

> ...je suis le hasard, la rupture, le signe! Je suis ton éma-
> nation et ton ange. Il n'y a qu'un abîme entre nous, qui
> ne sommes rien l'un sans l'autre.

In this ideal rape and hymen, the mind will take possession of its
body like an angel of light, a Flaming One — *Ignis sunt* —:

> J'apparaîtrai à mes membres comme un prodige, je chasserai
> l'impuissance de ma terre, j'occuperai mon empire jusqu'
> aux ongles, tes extrémités m'obéiront et nous entrerons har-
> diment dans le royaume de nos yeux.

Here we recall that the poet has rendered this act of love, in which
the self comes into self-possession, with the same vigorous eroticism
in "Aurore."

In "B" it is no longer a *moi* speaking, but a narrator who beholds
"l'être" — a body and a mind united — emerge from the vague
shrouds of bed and night. Only after the lucid awakening of the
entire being does the actual dialogue begin, the "colloque dans un
être" of body and mind. Such a colloquy is not rare in Valéry's
work. In another morning poem, "Chant de l'idée maîtresse" (*O*, I,
357-59), the master notion summons its "être" into being with a
similar vigor. And the matutinal exchange of "esprit" and "corps"

comprises one of Valéry's formal Dialogues, the "Colloque dans un être" (O, I, 360-66), which terminates in Teste's query, "la question la plus simple du monde: *Que peut un homme?*"

In the "C" poem, the *moi* confronting the world is composed of an inner tension of opposites which makes up its essence:

> Sur le balcon qui se propose au-dessus des feuilles, sur le seuil de la première heure et de tout ce qui est possible, je dors et je veille, je suis jour et nuit... L'âme s'abreuve à la source du temps, boit un peu de ténèbres, un peu d'aurore, se sent femme endormie, ange fait de lumière, se recueille, s'attriste, et s'enfuit sous forme d'oiseau jusqu'à la cime à demi nue dont le roc perce, chair et or, le plein azur nocturne. [8]

The matutinal Self, collected for future action and saddened by past weariness, is at once an angel of light and a woman sleeping, animus and anima.

The "A B C" poems, then, are a sequential series of three dramas, whose dramatic tension is produced by a multiple play of opposites — sleeping-waking, absence-presence, *corps-esprit, être-connaître, moi-monde*—. The Angel is the waking presence of the mind. All of these antitheses of the Self may be subsumed under the general dialectic of darkness and light, the shadowy unfathomable human reality and the bright, angelic inspiration and aspiration. As one element in this dialectical movement passes over into its opposite, it is *aufgehoben,* in the Hegelian sense of being fulfilled and preserved in it. For the notion of the world is meaningful only in and for a mind, *esprit* rising out of the *corps* by which it must be sustained: "C E M."

Yet the very phenomenon of a dialectic points to an intrinsic and insuperable duality within the self, and that of the self with the world. With his characteristic self-objectification, Valéry projects the "pure self" even beyond the very "esprit" of the C E M configuration, thereby recalling the triple fragmentation of the self in the "Anagogical Revelation." In a *Notebook* of his later years, he writes:

> Moi et CEM. Comme on a fini par distinguer plusieurs "masses," ainsi le faut-il faire entre les MOI. Il y en a autant

---

[8] Valéry, *Alphabet,* pp. 7-8 (but pages unnumbered in this edition).

qu'oppositions ou de NON-MOIS. Or j'en distingue au moins
3. Je me distingue (à tel moment d'une certaine évolution
fonctionnelle)—de MON CORPS, de MON ESPRIT, de MON
MONDE. Et ce qui se distingue des 3 est le MOI-PUR, l'équi-
distant et l'équidifférent par excellence—qu'il faut bien
désigner par un mot — Mais qui précède tous les mots.
(*Cahiers*, XXIII, 424)

In the *œuvre* the fundamental dualism manifests itself in the
Teste-Eupalinos dichotomy, on which Abraham Livni comments:
"...son problème sera d'associer et d'harmoniser les deux moitiés
de lui-même, le Teste qu'il continuera de porter en lui, et l'anti-
Teste dont il sait maintenant la primordiale importance." Livni
considers the Teste/anti-Teste dialectic "comme la clé de compré-
hension de Valéry." [9] He likewise observes that the agon underlying
all of Valéry's work is that of the angelic and the human selves:
"L'ange lumineux refuse l'obscurité de l'homme. Voilà le thème
central des pensées de Valéry, et la clé de son œuvre." [10] We intend
to show how it not merely informs, but also forms, that work.

Throughout the *œuvre,* as we have seen, Valéry's angelic aspirations are projected upon various symbolic figures, like Descartes,
Teste, Sémiramis, Leonardo; in the *Notebooks* they are frequently
represented by "Gladiator," the name of a famous race horse which
stands for that perfect "dressage" and discipline by which the self
masters and overcomes itself (its selves). "Gladiator. Il n'y a qu'une
chose à faire, se refaire. Ce n'est pas simple" (*Cahiers*, VIII, 182),
reads an entry from 1921; and a year later: "Gladiator, etc. Théorie
de la pureté et des synthèses. ...Qu'il y a deux *directions* dans
l'âme—L'une allant vers pureté et puis vers les constructions de cette
pureté; l'autre, allant vers le troublé et la confuse impureté" (*Cahiers*, VIII, 759). "Gladiator" is yet another name for "Ange; " and
the precious "dossier 'Ange,' " preserved at the Bibliothèque Nationale, bears the title "*Gladiator.*"

---

[9] Abraham Livni, *La Recherche du Dieu chez Paul Valéry* (Montréal:
Presses de l'Université de Montréal, 1978), p. 30.
[10] Ibid., p. 60.

CHAPTER VI

ANGELIC REFLECTIONS IN THE "NARCISSE" FRAGMENTS, "SÉMIRAMIS," AND "PARABOLES"

In Valéry's œuvre, one of the most obsessive symbolic figures for the divided self is that of "Narcisse." It appears first in the sonnet of September 1890 (O, I, 1554) which predates the poem the young Valéry had submitted to the judgment of Mallarmé; next in the "Fragments du Narcisse" of the early twenties which found their definitive form in *Charmes* of 1926; finally in the "Cantate du Narcisse," which the poet wrote in the late thirties "sur la commande de Mme Germaine Tailleferre pour servir de libretto à une cantate qui a été composée par cette éminente musicienne" (O, I, 403). When Valéry lectured "Sur les Narcisse" in 1941, he remarked that "ce thème de *Narcisse*...est une sorte d'auto-biographie poétique" (O, I, 1557), and recalled the famous tomb of Narcissa in the Botanical Garden at Montpellier which had inspired his early "Narcisse." The theme developed with the poet, and finally, in an important fusion, most fundamental to the poet's vision, merged with that of the Angel: "L'Ange - (au bord) de la fontaine," the title of the earliest draft of the prose poem "L'Ange," which became the poet's last work. From the first Narcissus sonnet to the "Fragments" and the early drafts of "The Angel," the theme had evolved during the thirty years in which the young and gifted Symbolist poet had developed into one of the great poets of his language and one of the most eminent intellectual figures of his time. And while the young poet had celebrated the theme in the traditional form of a sonnet, the mature Valéry developed it, significantly, in "Fragments."

From the outset, Valéry's Narcissus owes much more to Mallarmé's "Hérodiade," which he had read at the time he composed his early treatments of the theme, than to the Ovidian model. Both Mallarmé's and Valéry's protagonists seek in their mirror image a "purer" self for which they forsake the living world about them. In "Narcisse parle," however, the reflected image lacks the tragic dimension of the later Fragments, as the young Symbolist sings "Mon image de fleurs humides couronnée" in the familiar setting of the Sleeping Beauty's "bois dormant":

> Je t'adore, sous ces myrtes, ô l'incertaine
> Chair pour la solitude éclose tristement
> Qui se mire dans le miroir au bois dormant. (O, I, 83)

The "Fragments du Narcisse," which contains some of Valéry's most accomplished lyrics — consider, for example, the sunset passage of the first part (O, I, 123, lines 26-33) — consists of three numbered sections, making up the three acts of Narcissus' drama: the *moi*'s aspiration to embrace and comprehend his "inépuisable Moi"; the illusion and rejection of human love; finally, the aspiring self conquered by night and death. Yet, the poem never becomes *Gedankenlyrik,* as its themes are modulated so musically that the reader is left with the haunting melodies of this death-bound quest, rather than with distinct thoughts. And this "musical" effect was precisely the poet's aim. James Lawler, in the course of his discussion of the poem, quotes from a letter in which Valéry explains his intention: "Ce qui m'a particulièrement requis dans le *Second Narcisse,* c'est la combinaison de la période syntaxique et de cette structure musicale perpétuelle, le *vers.*" [1]

The lyrico-musical development of the Death motif — it is the leitmotif of the entire composition — reaches its crescendo in the last act. In the second act, human love, viewed with Leonardesque objectivity, had been condemned as illusory and mortal; now the solitary *moi,* itself threatened with extinction, clutches to its fading image in a terror which might recall for us Mallarmé's Igitur before his mirror in the "midnight chamber":

---

[1] Lawler, *Lecture de Valéry,* p. 101.

Toi seul, ô mon corps, mon cher corps,
Je t'aime, unique objet qui me défends des morts.

(O, I, 129)

Aspiring after transcendence and immortality, the Self is condemned to a temporal existence and a life of which death is an inherent
part. The motif of temporality is developed throughout the poem
by means of the beautiful melodies of sunset and nightfall over the
forest, and their reflection in the fountain. The *moi* is bound to both
the life and to the death of the surrounding world:

Bientôt va frissonner le désordre des ombres!
L'arbre aveugle vers l'arbre étend ses membres sombres,
Et cherche affreusement l'arbre qui disparaît...
Mon âme ainsi se perd dans sa propre forêt,
Où la puissance échappe à ses formes suprêmes...
L'âme, l'âme aux yeux noirs, touche aux ténèbres mêmes,
Elle se fait immense et ne rencontre rien...
Entre la mort et soi, quel regard est le sien! (O, I, 130)

A *Notebook* entry from the early twenties links the figure of
Narcissus again to his "corps" and its temporality: "Monologue de
Narcisse. Le *corps*. Objet, limite, serf et maître de la connaissance.
Lieu du bonheur et du malheur, du présent, du passé et de l'avenir"
(*Cahiers*, VII, 619); and a passage of the mid-20s reads: "Narcisse
N'est-ce point penser à la mort que se regarder au miroir? n'y
voit-on pas son périssable L'immortel y voit son mortel" (*Cahiers*,
X, 848). This becomes the theme of Valéry's last poem, which, as
we mentioned, began to take form with a fusion of the "Narcisse"
and the "Ange" figures in 1921. In the early sketch called "L'Ange—
(au bord) de la fontaine," an immortal being, "a kind of angel,"
confronts his mortal half in his reflected image: "Une sorte d'ange
était assis sur le bord d'une fontaine. Il se regardait et se voyait
homme, et en larmes, et en proie à une douleur [tristesse] infinie"
(*Cahiers*, VIII, 370).

Another angelic figure of Valéry's poetic universe is Sémiramis.
Sémiramis, the woman? No, Sémiramis, "enchanteresse et roi!" She
had preoccupied the poet for many years. Her origins go back to an
"abandoned, unfinished" poem of 1899,[2] and she first appeared in

---

2 Cf. Whiting, *Valéry jeune poète*, p. 147.

publication in 1920, under the title "Sémiramis (*Fragment d'un très ancien poème*)," which still lacked some of the stanzas that now make up the last piece of *Album de vers anciens*, "Air de Sémiramis" (*O*, I, 91-94), of 1920 and 1926. In 1934, Valéry wrote "Sémiramis mélodrame en trois actes et deux interludes" (*O*, I, 182-96), presented in May of that year at the Opéra de Paris, to the music of Arthur Honegger. Valéry's notions on opera and melodrama exceed the scope of this discussion; what concerns us here is the symbolic figure of Sémiramis, whose principal trait is *orgueil,* the angelic quality par excellence. Sémiramis' pride is superhuman, and literally projects her beyond the human and the living.

In both the poem and the melodrama, the queen's real lover is her god, the Sun, from her morning awakening in the poem to the consummation of their union at the closing of the melodrama. "...Existe! ...Sois enfin toi-même! dit l'Aurore," summoning Sémiramis to reject, like the Parque, the enticements of her body:

> Et débarrasse-toi d'un désordre de drames
> Qu'engendrent sur ton lit les monstres de ton sang! (*O*, I, 91)

Sémiramis *rises* to meet her lover: "je vole au-devant du soleil!" Throughout the poem, her angelic aspirations are expressed in verbs stressing vertical tension, "je surgis," "il m'emporte," "je vole," "la fraiche/Altitude m'appelle"; they suggest, in fact, a winged creature:

> Monte, ô Sémiramis, maîtresse d'une spire
> Qui d'un cœur sans amour s'élance au seul honneur! (*O*, I, 92)

In the melodrama's third act, Sémiramis, echoed by the chorus, sings her soaring aspiration:

> Altitude, mon Altitude, mon Ciel,
> ... ...
> Temple du Ciel, je chante tes loua*nges*
> La Colombe sur toi s'élève
> A la hauteur de l'Aigle
> Sur la Hauteur, que je m'enivre d'astres! [my emphasis]

Mounting the parapet, she rises toward the altar she has built to the Sun: "Que je respire ici la domination toute pure! ...il n'y a point de Tour si haute que je puisse de sa hauteur découvrir les bornes de mon âme"; she prostrates herself upon it, praying to be taken up into the ultimate "pureté du Non-être," and consumed by its fire:

> —A présent,—je me coucherai sur la pierre de cet Autel, et je prierai le Soleil, bientôt dans toute sa force, qu'il me réduise en vapeur et en cendres, afin que de moi-même et de l'instant,—se dégage cette Colombe que j'ai nourrie de tant de gloire et de tant d'orgueil. (O, I, 196)

Her prayer is heard: "une colombe s'envole. L'Autel vide brille au soleil."

Sémiramis reaches — and crosses over — that "borne," the extreme limit from which there is no return. It is precisely the cyclical returns of the natural — the temporal — order that she conquers in her blazing ascension. For the angelic *orgueil* rebels against the endless repetitions imposed by a body and its appurtenance to Nature. The angelic aspiration projects the *moi* beyond the space-time limitations of human reality, the particularization and individuation that tie the mind to a specific human life with its history and personality, and condemn it to a Nietzschean "ewige Wiederkunft." Zarathustra had sighed: "Ach, der Mensch kehrt wieder! Der kleine Mensch kehrt ewig wieder! "[3] And this human fate which Zarathustra accepts — "amor fati" — the Angel rejects.

But Teste knows that he was deluding himself when he prayed, "donnez... donnez la suprême pensée..." (O, II, 37), he knows that he cannot reach beyond life without annihilating the life of his very mind. "La vie," says Valéry,

> s'oppose à l'intelligence par sa forme périodique, l'intelligence est du type 'une fois pour toutes,'

and

> l'esprit (le plus esprit de l'esprit) répugne à la répétition. Résume—épuise—cherche la loi pour se débarasser des faits, du nombre, du prévu. Ce qui est prévu l'accable. Tout ce qui recommence lui semble 'bêtise,' donc la 'vie'...Je t'ai

---

[3] Friedrich Nietzsche, *Werke in Zwei Bänden* I (München: Carl Hanser Verlag, 1976), p. 699.

vécu mille fois (Heure), car trois fois valent mille et dix
mille pour Moi, l'Esprit... (*Cahiers*, XIV, 574; and XXVI,
291)

Ned Bastet, in connection with Valéry's last alter-angel figure, his
Faust, has analyzed this opposition of "esprit" to the cyclical operation of the nature of which it is a part.[4]

In rejecting Eros, the spirit refuses to perpetuate the race and its
own imprisonment in the cycle of nature, of which it is, as Valéry
repeatedly insists, a part: Schopenhauer redivivus! Sémiramis had
killed her earthly lover, the beautiful captive, and had then risen
toward the sun; the Young Fate, in a lucid moment of her night,
had refused to participate in Nature's universal rhythm:

> Et ces bords sinueux, ces plis et ces calices,
> Pour que la vie embrasse un autel de délices,
> Où mêlant l'âme étrange aux éternels retours,
> La sémence, le lait, le sang coulent toujours?
> Non! L'horreur m'illumine, exécrable harmonie!
>
> (*O*, I, 104)

Nearly identical, one recalls, was also the refusal of Mallarmé's Hérodiade: "Du reste, je ne veux rien d'humain" — immediately before
the melting of the diamond.

One of the "Petits poèmes abstraits" which Valéry published in
1932 in *La Revue de France*, entitled significantly "L'Unique," again
celebrates the tension between the spirit's angelic aspiration to transcend, and its contrary vital dependence on, Time, that is, "Être." Its
concluding paragraph juxtaposes the *moi*'s "états exceptionnels"
with the regular, rhythmic breathing and heartbeats that tie it to
the world:

> Mais tandis que le moment même de l'esprit aspire à
> ce qui lui semble sans exemple, et que j'espère en des états
> exceptionnels, chaque battement de mon cœur redit, chaque
> souffle de ma bouche rappelle—*que la chose la plus impor-
> tante est celle qui se répète le plus.*

---

[4] Ned Bastet, "Faust et le cycle" in *Entretiens sur Paul Valéry* (La Haye
et Paris: Mouton, 1968), pp. 115-28.

And a passage from *Mélange,* which plays a variation on the theme of the Fallen Angel, reads:

> Un esprit allait voir cesser son état; il devait tomber de l'éternité dans le Temps, s'incarner:
> "Tu vas *vivre!* "
> C'était *mourir* pour lui. Quel effroi! Descendre dans le Temps! (*O,* I, 299)

A prose "Psalm" from a 1925 Notebook, entitled "Bice—Ange" [Bice is Béatrice], retells the story of the Fallen Angel and explicitly identifies the *moi* with the angel fallen into space and time:

> Bice—Ange.
> Psaume.
> Je ne suis pas où vous me voyez. Je ne suis pas où vous croyez. Vous aimez, vous haïssez un fantôme. ...De loin, j'anime cet homme qui est présent pour vous.
> —Un ange fut jeté par quelque Faute de... dans le corps d'un homme. La Mémoire de sa condition première lui fut ôtée.
> Qu'est-ce qu'une âme qui a perdu la mémoire? Il ne gardait de l'ange que le sentiment de n'être pas ce qu'il était, car le sentiment angélique de l'*ubiquité* ne s'était pas aboli étant ineffaçable.
> *Etre en quelque lieu,* en *quelque temps,* condition humaine, il la subissait, mais ne pouvait s'y accoutumer et il était toujours malheureux...
> Enfin *Moi*—C'est un portrait... (*Cahiers,* X, 721)

In a 1942 *Notebook,* under the *Ego* heading, Valéry projects a "treatise" on angels, and his notes on the project summarize many of the traits we have been tracing in his angelology, whether explicitly stated as such, or implied. For, as we have seen, the Valéryan Angel frequently appears wearing the masks of Gladiator, Teste, Leonardo, Narcissus, Sémiramis and others. Here, again, the text identifies the self with the angelic:

> Traités singuliers.
> A.   De la représentation des êtres incorporels— ...
> B.   Racoler tous les textes où il est question des *anges,* depuis Babylone, etc. et en faire un recueil.
> J'entends tous les textes sérieusement écrits—par des gens qui croyaient ce qu'ils disaient.

C. Des anges—secundum Paul Valéry.   Ego
(Pierre [Pierre Louÿs] n'aimait pas ce nom…Ridicule
1830 pour lui. Moi (91) lui donnais un autre son—c'étaient
des "esprits" *implacables*—intelligences sans défaut, por-
teurs de la fatalité—de la Lumière mentale. Je voyais toute
une *mythologie de l'esprit*—la conscience opérante—qui
transforme et consume tout ce qu'elle attaque. [Here a
marginal note refers to: "*Le Solitaire* dans Faust II et
Teste, Léonard, etc."] Une sorte d'idéal de ma volonté et
de ma réaction 92 contre sensibilité exagérée—qui m'a fait
tant souffrir. Ceci s'est modifié vers 192…
    Leur rigueur pénétrante du rayon. Cf. final de *Sémira-
mis*— — Réaction.

The entry's following paragraphs point to a development of the angel
theme that we discussed in connection with "Eupalinos," that of the
sublimation of Eros to the angelic "esprit créateur," which was in-
creasingly to preoccupy the poet's later years and which became one
of the major motifs of *Mon Faust*:

> D'où d'étranges combinaisons avec les sources de ten-
> dresse—et de chant secret—Et toute une vie dans le rêve
> d'une intimité dans l'extrême du sentir—créateur. Avoir
> pour Idole l'absence d'idoles. Aller au bout des puissances
> du seul—à deux. *Reconstituer l'amour dans l'au-delà des
> états connus et prévus.*
>   —Et *vivre une fois pour toutes.* Ceci mène à tenter de
> découvrir, dégager, éliminer *tout ce qui se répète, ou ré-
> pète*—D'où bien des recherches.
>   Et *c'est tout Moi*—Et c'était vouloir me réduire à un
> Ange + Bête = *non Homme,* cette chose *impure.* (*Cahiers,*
> XXV, 802)

We have been tracing the evolution of the angelic self in Valéry's
thought and its many manifestations in the œuvre. The sublimation
of love to the angelic, which had been a preoccupation of the poet
from the twenties on, is mirrored in the unpublished manuscripts of
"L'Ange et l'amour," in the Cahier *Gladiator* (1920-1925) preserved
at the Bibliothèque Nationale, and the theme was then transmuted
to become *matière* for the great work of Valéry's later years, the
Faust fragments. But Valéry constructs his "Mythology of the Mind"
throughout his creative life, and its hero is the Angel. That Angel —
like fire, *ignis sunt* — transforms what he touches, and rejects

Nature's "ewige Wiederkunft," "tout ce qui se répète." However, in the end, the "esprit angélique" is unable to overcome the inherent duality of *homo duplex* and condemns the human as "impure." Valéry, we noted, will remain essentially a Cartesian dualist all his life.

One year after the *mélodrame* "Sémiramis," in 1935, Valéry wrote a series of free-verse "Paraboles" (*O*, I, 197-201) to accompany twelve watercolors by L. Albert-Lasard, texts which constitute poetic variations on the "ange-bête" or "connaître-être" dichotomy. Part of the text appeared, with very slight modifications, in *Mélange* under the title "Psaume devant la bête" (*O*, I, 356-57). One of the epigraphs of the "Parables" is Pascal's "L'Homme n'est ni ange ni bête"; the other and major epigraph consists of the three last lines of one of the most famous poems of Rilke's *Neue Gedichte*, "Die Flamingos."

Loulou Albert-Lasard had met Rilke in 1914 and had soon become a very close friend of the poet, one of whose best-known portraits she painted in 1916. The epigraph of "Paraboles" also discreetly commemorates the friendship of Valéry and Rilke, ardent on the part of Rilke, and cut short by his untimely death. But the subtitle of "Die Flamingos," reproduced in the epigraph, "Jardin des Plantes," also serves to set the stage of "Paraboles," the Garden of Eden:

> Quand il n'y avait encore que l'Ange et l'Animal dans ce Jardin
> ......
> Et quand Dieu, et les Choses, et les Anges et les Animaux
> Et la Lumière qui est Archange
> Étaient tout ce qui était,
> CE FUT L'ÈRE DE PURETÉ.

The animal is as pure as the angel, as pure as the light of the angels in their traditional celestial hierarchies:

> Pur était le Lion, et pure la Fourmi,
> Pur le Taureau et pure la Couleuvre;
> Pur le Dragon, et pures les Vertus
> Et les Trônes et les Très hautes Hiérarchies;

For purity and order are paradise before the Fall, and the Fall is personified in *homo duplex,* that creature made up of "esprit" *and* "corps." The Garden's—the poem's—MOI is a pure reflector, a mirror whose clear surface "trembles" at the sight of Man:

ET MOI, je connaissais tout ceci
Avec une netteté extrême et extraordinaire;
......
Comme les yeux de mon esprit réfléchissaient cette pureté,
Subissaient, comme le miroir d'une eau calme,
L'ordre et l'éclat de toutes choses sans défaut,
Sans nulle idée,
Voici: d'entre les feuilles une Figure vint.
......
Et celui-ci n'était "Ni Ange ni Bête".
LE MIROIR de ma présence simple se rida
......
Sur le miroir d'éternelle durée
De mon ravissement
Fut un frémissement:
......
HOMME fut cet événement:
Tel est le nom que je te donne.
JE SAVAIS comme en LUI qu'il n'était ANGE ni BÊTE:
Je le connus par une souffrance sans pareille.

Man appears, then, under a sign of pain and sorrow unknown in the Garden, and in this "incomparable suffering" the mirror of consciousness, the poem's persona, recognizes its kinship with the creature that has destroyed the original order and harmony:

Mais CELUI-CI n'était ni l'un ni l'autre:
Je le savais d'une science immédiate et très certaine:
Une science de souffrance, une souffrance de science
Entre lesquelles
Le silence de l'HOMME et le silence mien
Changeaient d'âme à chaque instant...

Conscience, "connaître," and "l'HOMME" are one, and now apostrophize the Angels, the pure Light, and the Pure Acts "a little higher than my highest self":

ANGE, disait en moi Celui dont je possédais si bien la présence,
ANGES, leur disait-il,
Merveilles éternelles de l'amour et de la lumière,
Actes purs

O seulement connaissables par le désir
Par l'espoir, par l'orgueil, par l'amour,
Par tout ce qui est
Présence d'absence,
Toutefois Vous m'êtes mystères qui brillez
Un peu au-dessus du plus haut degré de moi-même...

This hymn to the Angels reflects related motifs we have discussed earlier: the Angels as Light and Pure Act, and the concept of presence in absence. But then the separated Self laments his Fall from Paradise and the pure happiness of Angels *and* of Animals. The Angel(s) — each a species to himself — is "knowable" to the Self by his own desire, hope, pride and love, finally by a Mallarméan presence that is absence. For the Angel is not a reality, not an article of faith, but rather an Ideal and guiding principle of the Self. An entry dated the year of "Paraboles" explains: "...le principe de l'Ange est transcendance en pureté. Il commande de ne pas confondre. Ce qui est menaçant pour la 'foi.' Car la foi est confusion des *forces* que l'on prête à une image et de celles que l'on éprouverait de la présence du modèle de cette image" (*Cahiers,* XVII, 750). Like Rilke's God, Valéry's Angel here is a direction, rather than an object, of desire; and this angelic force estranges from its human nature the mind it attracts. [5] But most often, Valéry's Angel is internalized, as the human is rejected. In a 1936 notation, marked "Ange," the poet exclaims: "tout ce qui est *humain* m'est étranger...Quoi de plus étrange au regard de l'esprit que de se trouver être 'un homme,' un mortel, un mammifère, un semblable...!" (*Cahiers,* XIX, 138). Each angel, we noted, is a species to himself and thus cannot have a "semblable," according to Saint Thomas and to Valéry. We recall that Thomistic angelology influenced the poet's. An entry of the "Cahier B 1910," the year in which Valéry had attended lectures on the *Summa,* reads: "Selon Thomas d'Aquin, l'Aevum est au Temps, ce que l'esprit ou l'ange est à la créature corporelle" (p. 581).

---

[5] Cf. my "The Angel in Valéry and Rilke," *Comparative Literature,* 35 (Summer 1983), 119-50.

CHAPTER VII

EROS AND *NOUS*

Beginning with the early twenties, from the time of the composition of "Eupalinos," the gravitational force which arrests the "transcendance en pureté" of Valéry's Angel is human love; and the harmonizing of the mysterious forces of Eros with the purity of the Angelic, of *être* with *connaître*, without sacrificing or compromising either, constitutes the dramatic conflict of much of Valéry's mature work. Significantly, "L'Ange et l'amour" remains "unfinished."

In the dossier "Ange" at the Bibliothèque Nationale, under the cover of the "Cahier *Gladiator* 1920-1925" is a small red notebook, written in ink in Valéry's beautiful handwriting, entitled "L'Ange et l'amour." [1] On the fourth page of the Notebook, the entry reads:

> L'Ange à la fontaine
> L'ange Ghimmel se sent humaniser
> il ne comprend pas ce qui lui survient
> va visiter la terre, etc.

In this "ange à la fontaine" we recognize the Angel of Valéry's last poem, some of whose successive drafts are also in the "Ange" dossier. But "L'Ange et l'amour" projects the angel's descent—or is it a Fall?—(in)to human love. At the beginning of every other page of the Notebook, the successively numbered notations indicate the motifs, or themes, to be developed. This produces an impression

---

[1] I wish to express my special gratitude to Mme Florence de Lussy of the Bibliothèque Nationale for permitting me to examine the dossier "Ange" during my stay in Paris 1978-79 in connection with the preparation of this study.

of musico-lyrical variations, so that the work might have become a "mélodrame" in the Valéryan sense of that term.

As night falls, the Angel finds himself on earth, where his singing is met by that of the birds, whose song and freedom of movement always fascinated the poet.[2] In contrast to the birds, Man appears "heavy and sad," and the notations read: "(Peinture des hommes) ...ceux qui ont un corps lourd et douloureux mais qui vivent en-tr'eux." "L'homme lui paraît dans son effort." Then follow some Latin notations on the intellectual nature of the angels (the Thomistic influence we already pointed to in our discussion), and "Désespoir/de n'être qu'une/pensée/corps glorieux/éternel message/jamais pour/soi-même." This motif then modulates into a sort of elegiac chant, a song of the Angel's solitude. The song is heard, and on the following double page we find "Celle qui entend le chant. ...Extase, Hyp-nose. A genoux. Vibration de sa chair. ..." Her whole being rever-berates to that unheard-of song. On the following pages, she goes to sleep; and upon reawakening, all has changed about her, and she sees each thing anew. Now a vision of "les amours ordinaires" makes her sad. Gradually, the Angel's and the Woman's song begin to form an antiphonal call and response, so that they meet in song — in poetry — before coming face to face. Notations suggest their emo-tions, the Woman's "gaité inexplicable" and the "tristesse de l'Ange." Their meeting is marked by "Accueil - Repas du soir Bains Visitation Danse — Elle sert son repas; " and then they walk silently among the flowers. In the culminating pages of the project, after the emo-tions of tenderness, the desire to yield to life and "corps," comes a "Scène" of "Fire, Kiss," and the "Création du corps de l'ange." Then, after "infinite gratitude," and "liberation," and of "Ten-dresse - le Trop," follows the transformation through love, its "mys-tique, émerveillement," and finally a scene under a tree and a "chant de l'Arbre." On the last page (35), the note: "Bain. Le corps." The remainder of the notebook is empty.

To our knowledge Valéry never developed "L'Ange et l'amour; " his last Angel is the solitary one by the Fountain. What might have been — had it been possible for the poet to harmonize human love

---

[2] Cf. Christine M. Crow, *Paul Valéry: Consciousness of Nature* (Cam-bridge: Cambridge University Press, 1972), esp. pp. 104-6, "Living Things."

and angelic purity — may perhaps be suggested by another "Chant
de l'Arbre," Tityre's "chant" of love which he calls "un premier
temps d'un poème futur":

> AMOUR n'est rien qu'il ne croisse à l'extrême:
> Croître est sa loi; il meurt d'être le même,
> Et meurt en qui ne meure point d'amour.
> Vivant de soif toujours inassouvie,
> Arbre dans l'âme aux racines de chair
> Qui vit de vivre au plus vif de la vie
> Il vit de tout, du doux et de l'amer
> Et du cruel, encor mieux que du tendre.
> Grand Arbre Amour, qui ne cesses d'étendre
> Dans ma faiblesse une étrange vigueur,
> Mille moments que se garde le cœur
> Te sont feuillage et flèches de lumière!
> Mais cependant qu'au soleil du bonheur
> Dans l'or du jour s'épanouit ta joie,
> Ta même soif, qui gagne en profondeur,
> Puise dans l'ombre, à la source des pleurs...
> (O, II, 182-83)

This most beautiful Love song of Valéry's last years, from the "Dialogue de l'Arbre" of 1943, harmonizes the Dionysian Eros — "aux
racines de chair" — and its Apollonian sublimation — "dans l'or du
jour" — in one of the poet's favorite symbolic images, the Tree of
Life, "Grand Arbre Amour," rooted deep in the earth and reaching
up high toward the sun, dualistic image par excellence.

In 1941, Valéry published *Études pour "Mon Faust,"* in subsequent editions entitled *"Mon Faust" (Ébauches),* containing the
fragments *Lust, La Demoiselle de Cristal,* and *Le Solitaire ou les
malédictions d'univers, Féerie dramatique (O,* II, 276-403). In the
preface, addressed to the "lecteur de bonne foi et de mauvaise volonté," the author tells us: "or, un certain jour de 1940, je me suis
surpris me parlant à deux voix et me suis laissé aller à écrire ce qui
venait." He goes on to mention a "vaguely" projected "Faust III,"
which:

> pourrait comprendre un nombre indéterminé d'ouvrages plus
> ou moins faits pour le théâtre: drames, comédies, tragédies,
> féeries selon l'occasion; ...mais, qui, je le savais, n'existe-
> raient jamais... Mais c'est ainsi que de scène en scène, d'acte

en acte, se sont composés ces trois quarts de *Lust* et ces
deux tiers du *Solitaire* qui sont réunis dans ce volume.
(*O,* II, 276-77)

The last "fourth" or act of *Lust* and the final "third" of the *Solitaire*
were, to our knowledge, never completed.

Valéry's notations on drama, as well as the relationship of his
Faust to that of Goethe, lie outside of the scope of our discussion. [3]
The figure of Faust which occupied the poet for many years, as borne
out by *Notebook* entries as early as the twenties, concerns us as another reflection of the Angelic Self. For the *Faust* fragments are the
expression of a mounting tension between the two members of the
Eros-Nous dichotomy; Valéry makes yet another attempt to reconcile the two, to transform the one into the other in *Lust,* while in
the Solitaire he brings the conflict between *être* and *connaître* to its
dramatic climax. The *Lust* fragment, as its name suggests, deals with
Love; the *Solitaire* presents the confrontation of an essentially Cartesian Faust and an antagonist who is one of his own extremes, a
dehumanized absurdity who might well be, as Kurt Weinberg has
suggested, a caricature of Pascal, one of whose *Pensées* (number 358)
is that "le malheur veut que qui veut faire l'ange fait la bête."
The Solitaire does, in fact, turn into a howling wolf as he precipitates
Faust into the abyss.

In *Lust,* the theme of Eros is introduced when Faust's secretary,
Lust, reads back to him what he had previously dictated. She comes
to the phrase "Érôs énergumène" which the "Maître" does not
remember at all. In fact, Mephistopheles had slipped it into Lust's
notes, but Faust — incidentally demonstrating a principle of literary
influence — likes it and "takes" it: "Érôs énergumène?... Ce n'est
pas possible! ... Ceci n'est pas de moi. Mais ce n'est pas mal. Érôs
énergumène!... Ceci doit être de moi. .. je le prends! Érôs énergumène. Érôs en tant que source d'extrême énergie...je vois ce que
j'en puis faire! " (*O,* II, 282).

---

[3] For the former, cf. Huguette Laurenti's thesis *Paul Valéry et le théâtre*
(Paris: Gallimard, 1973); for the latter, Kurt Weinberg's brilliant analysis of
The Figure of Faust in Valéry and Goethe: An Exegesis of "Mon Faust" (Prin-
ceton: Princeton University Press, 1976).

Valéry called Faust's secretary "Lust," for she embodies both "delight" and "pleasure," while also recalling another Faust and his Gretchen. "Oh," exclaims Lust, "le joli titre!... La Demoiselle de Cristal! ...un beau nom, Lust de Cristal," Faust retorting: "méritez-le! Devenez transparente" (*O,* II, 287). But when the old Mephistopheles offers his services to the Master, to help things along with "un rien d'énergumène, une esquisse d'Érôs," Faust turns him down, as he does love: "point d'amour; je sais trop qu'il s'achève en ruine, en dégoût, en désastre," and we recall the second act of the "Fragments du Narcisse." Faust only wants what Mephistopheles would not understand anyhow: "mais je te le redis, je ne veux qu'une présence douce auprès de ma pensée" (*O,* II, 292). Being a spirit, though a fallen one, the devil is too simple — pure? — to understand the demands of the human heart: "tu appliques une science du cœur tout élémentaire," says Faust, "d'une simplicité tout angélique, illustrée plutôt que secourue, par quelques tours de physique amusante, toujours un peu les mêmes" (*O,* II, 300). Besides, the old Devil is not up to modern times. "Just imagine," Faust explains, "they have even reinvented the old Chaos," whereupon poor Mephistopheles cries out: "Ils ont retrouvé le CHAOS... J'étais Archange!" In a brave new world, "beyond good and evil," both heaven and hell have lost their old importance, and the outdated Devil thinks it really a great loss: "Mais pauvres gens! le Mal était si beau, jadis...J'en étais l'Intelligence et le Principe" (*O,* II, 304).

The second act introduces the traditional disciple who has come from afar to meet the great Faust; he is carrying with him one of Faust's "immortal" works: "ce Traité extraordinaire du 'Corps de l'Esprit' qui ne me quitte pas." But the Master sends him away with the advice: "Prenez garde à l'amour" (*O,* II, 313), after which the angered and disappointed Disciple goes to the devil, whose demons (Bélial, Astaroth, Goungoune) would have gotten the better of him, had not a compassionate Lust saved him in the end. He falls in love with her — Mephistopheles' doing — but she, "la Demoiselle de Cristal," of course loves Faust, "ce grand seigneur de l'esprit."

One evening, dictating in the garden, Faust offers Lust a rose; then he ceases dictating: "Mais non... Je ne dicte pas...J'existe. Il fait divin, ce soir. Trop bon, trop doux, trop beau, même...la

Terre est tendre... C'est trop pour un seul..." The enchanted Lust says: "mais c'est vous qui chantez, mon Maître... Vous paraissez un dieu, ce soir.." With Lust — his desire — in the evening garden, Faust gives up thinking for living, and his very words become the poetry we know:

> Je vous dis que je ne pense à rien. ...mon corps ne sait pas encore, et mon esprit ne me dit rien. Seule, chante cette heure, la profusion du soir.

The last sentence, an alexandrine, signals the climax of *Lust,* as Faust walks through the soft evening with Lust among the flowers, in a scene which suggests what the unwritten portion of "L'Ange et l'amour" might have become. Faust abandons himself to *être:*

> VIVRE... je ressens, je respire mon chef-d'œuvre. ... VI-VRE!... JE RESPIRE. N'est-ce pas tout? ...JE SUIS, n'est-ce pas extraordinaire?

Lust approaches Faust and puts her hand on his shoulder, saying:

> L'heure est trop mûre, trop chargée de fruits mûrs d'un jour de pleine splendeur pour qu'il se puisse que deux êtres, même si différents, ne soient pas mêmement à bout de leur résistance à la force des choses. (*O,* II, 318-23)

After this reenactment of the unwritten scene of "The Angel and Love," Lust offers Faust the forbidden fruit, amply foreshadowed earlier with the phrase "too charged with ripe fruit": "Viens," Faust first invites her to

> faire un tour dans le jardin que la nuit déjà brouille, et dont les ténèbres et les arbres nous attirent là-bas à leur douceur confuse...

Lust:

> Avec joie—"Lust"—Mais j'ai une soif! ...Permettez-moi de cueillir d'abord cette belle pêche...[*Elle cueille le fruit, y mord, le tend mordu à Faust.*] Oh! qu'elle est bonne, et puis... elle est à vous... Et puis, encore à moi... [*Faust la prend, y mord, la rend et regarde Lust. Elle lui prend le bras, ils sortent par la gauche*]." (*O,* II, p. 331)

In the following scene, we see Mephistopheles falling from a tree, a serpent, hissing "encore une affaire de Frruitt. ...."; but he understands nothing, and certainly not Lust's heart.

We must continue our plot summary to the third act, where Mephistopheles concedes to Lust: "Le Diable sera franc. Votre cœur m'embarrasse. Il m'intrigue parfois, comme parfois me déconcertent l'extrême intelligence et la lucidité excessive de Faust." How could he, the old Devil, understand the human heart, obscure even to Lust herself? Eros is his business, but Tenderness is beyond the reach of Satan — and of the Angels, as Rilke, too, asserts. Lust, the *ewig Weibliche,* has won the round against the Angels, both "the sons of light" and the Fallen One:

> Mon cœur vous soit obscur!... Il me l'est à moi-même. Tout démon que vous êtes, vous n'y pouvez rien comprendre. Après tout, vous n'êtes que le Diable. ... Il n'y a point de musique en vous... O mon cœur, tu te moques du mal... prendre... Ils sont purs, ils sont durs, ils sont forts. Mais les Anges eux-mêmes, les Archanges fidèles, tous ces fils de lumière et ces puissances de ferveur ne peuvent pas comprendre... Ils sont purs, ils sont durs, ils sont forts. Mais la tendresse!... Que voulez-vous que des êtres éternels puissent sentir le prix d'un regard, d'un instant, tout le don de la faiblesse... le don d'un bien qu'il faut saisir entre le naître et le mourir. Ils ne sont que lumière et tu n'es que ténèbres... Mais moi, mais nous, nous portons nos clartés et nous portons nos ombres... (O, II, 349)

A Notebook entry from 1941 confirms the doctrine of Lust's speech to the devil: "Faust III Satan et l'Archange. Ni l'un et l'autre comprennent rien à l'homme. Ils sont esprits. Ils sont purs, l'un dans le Bien l'autre dans le Mal..." And by extension, the *moi angélique* cannot understand himself, that is his own "other half," the human. "Enfin," continues the note:

> Faust considère l'homme entre Ange et Bête mais mélange et non combinaison il cherche à devenir combinaison à garder les caractères qui lui agréent et à supprimer les autres. Mais ceci est impossible? Il demeure pourtant en soi 'la distance infinie entre l'esprit et le corps.' L'esprit ne comprenant rien au corps, et ses rapports avec lui demeurant ceux d'ennemis ou victime la mort — l'amour. (*Cahiers,* XXIV, 51)

Lust, to which Valéry usually refers as "Faust III," in the *Note-books,* was his vain attempt to reconcile the two, and it had to be abandoned, unfinished like "L'Ange et l'amour."

Another notation from the same period again sets forth the problem: "Faust III Comment 'l'esprit' voit l'acte d'amour? ... Il faudrait dans *Lust,* un accès dans F. qui opérât la transformation (en scène) de l'état Érôs à l'état Nous avec vue transcendante de l'action d'amour (comme la section anatomique de Léonard)"; and the remainder of the entry suggests what the fourth act of *Lust* might have been, could it have been written: "Puis... (peut-être) retour—En somme, l'enchantement rompu—la scène de Lebwohl—à moins de la placer après quelque faute de la Lust; ni même faute mais qui brise l'édifice cristallin—*tout harmonique*" (*Cahiers,* XXIV, 16). Thus the final act would have been tragic, the downfall of the couple, the failure of the attempted marriage of "esprit" and "corps" in the mythopoetic figures of Faust and Lust. It would, in fact, have been Valéry's singular interpretation of the story of the Fall.

Ned Bastet's critical presentation of a wealth of "textes inédits: Quatrième acte de 'Lust' "[4] shows how profoundly Valéry was pre-occupied with this dramatic project, whose dominant theme is that of the transformation of "ordinary love" into "le grand amour" that would reconcile the warring halves of the Self, the "terrible angels" of the "Révélation anagogique." In one of the drafts, entitled "Der Dritte Faust," Lust, in a long monologue, likens the transformation of love to the alchemist's transmutation of base metal into gold; but for the "demoiselle de cristal" the supreme love is, of course, an "amour diamant." Lust, Faust's crystal-clear mirror, reflects his angelic aspirations:

> O Maître, faut-il, moi, que je t'instruise?...je vois, je vis de voir la suprême transmutation... celle de l'amour com-mune en amour diamant. C'est là le Grand-Œuvre. Tout ce qui n'est pas pour cet Œuvre et vers lui, en fait d'amour et de souci, me semble du déjà-vécu, déjà-voulu, subi, con-nu; déjà-porté; on a déjà joui, souffert, joué ce jeu, ce

---

4 Ned Bastet, "Textes inédits Quatrième acte de 'Lust' " in *Cahiers Paul Valéry II: "Mes théâtres"* (Paris: Gallimard, 1977), pp. 51-158.

rôle, cette vie. On s'y voit répétant, imitant, ressentant les
émois, les ardeurs ... les reprises. C'est ce Moi que je hais
et ne veux pas qui soit Moi... Mais Toi, mon Faust, toi
seul m'as fait connaître ou croire que tout autre pourrait
être le destin d'une amour. [5]

Lust's words, we said, reflect Faust and his *moi angélique,* one of
whose most fundamental conflicts with the human condition is that
of the body's repetitions or "reprises," the very life-rhythm that
ties the Self to Nature, and which "l'esprit" rejects. The very essence
of the life-perpetuating Eros is the "ewige Wiederkunft des Glei-
chen; " and it is this love, which resembles another and all others,
that the angelic lover refuses. [6] The "ultimate" lovers are logically
condemned to death — like Tristan and Iseut — for, like Sémiramis,
they must cross over that "boundary," the extreme limit from which
alone there is no return, no *Wiederkunft.*

Bastet finds that the "souvenir de Tristan" haunts the projected
forth act of *Lust;* he presents drafts in which Faust and Lust, like
the Wagnerian lovers, "chantent" their unique death-bound love as
a sublimation of life into art and poetry. Biblical echoes abound, as
in the following fragment with its overt allusion to the "*eritis sicut
dii*" (Genesis, III, 5):

> Nous serions comme les dieux—harmoniques intelligents,
> dans une correspondance directe de nos vies sensitives sans
> paroles et nos esprits feraient l'amour l'un avec l'autre
> comme les corps le peuvent faire. Cet accord harmonique
> serait plus qu'un accord de pensée—l'accomplissement.
> N'est-ce pas le sommet de la Poésie qui n'est après tout que
> tentative de communion? [7]

But it would end in a "farewell," and there is a "Lebwohl" scene
in which Faust laments: "Ô Lust, c'est toi que j'aurais chosie... J'y
vois trop clair. J'y vois trop clair! hélas! Rien d'humain ne m'est
plus. Et presque tout l'humain m'est étranger. [8] There the Valéryan

---

[5] Ibid., pp. 57-58.
[6] Bastet has, as we have mentioned, analyzed this conflict in "Faust et
le cycle"; cf. Chapter VI, Note 4.
[7] Bastet, "Inédits Quatrième acte de 'Lust'," p. 82.
[8] Ibid., p. 77.

Moi pur, speaking through the mask of retreating Faust, conveys a mordant inversion of Terence's warmly human "humani nil a me alienum! ": *Angelus sum: humani nil mihi familiarem puto.* A *Notebook* entry cited by Bastet confirms the defeat of Eros by Nous, the failure of the grand attempt to transform the one into the other, and the Pyrrhic victory of the *moi angélique:*

> L'acte IV aura eu pour but d'épuiser' la tentation de l'Érôs et d'aller jusqu'au bout de ses maléfices, avant de restituer Faust au vide désespéré et triomphant de la conscience qui a déjoué tous les pièges de la vie, et le plus périlleux de tous, 'le piège épouvantable de la tendresse'. [9]

It is this Faust, "restored to the desperate and triumphant void" of his angelic *Moi pur,* who, at the end of *Le Solitaire,* refuses the ultimate temptation, the enticements of the "Fées," to "start all over again" with life:

> Non, non... N'égarez point vos complaisances, Fées...
> Si grands soient les pouvoirs que l'on m'a découverts,
> Ils ne me rendront pas le goût de l'Univers.
> Le souci ne m'est point de quelque autre aventure,
> Moi qui sus l'ange vaincre et le démon trahir,
> J'en sais trop pour aimer, j'en sais trop pour haïr,
> Et je suis excédé d'être une créature. (*O,* II, 402)

* * *

A great angelic text contemporary with the *Faust* fragments is the tale of the Angel's visitation of the couple, of "Elihu" and "la fille de Chanaan." It appears in the twenty-fourth *Notebook (Cahiers,* XXIV, 21-23), which contains the many entries on "Faust III," under the Greek letters Theta and Epsilon-rho. Theta usually designates Valéry's reflections on religion in the *Notebooks,* while Epsilon-rho marks the "Eros" passages. Certain passages, explains Judith Robinson, [10] "portent deux signes: $\Sigma \rho$ et θ. Le θ évoque ici le rapport dans l'esprit de Valéry entre l'amour le plus intense et l'acuité d'une experience mystique." [11] In the tale of Elihu, the

---

[9] Ibid., p. 106.

[10] Judith Robinson, one of the foremost Valéry scholars, and whose work we have quoted above (Chap. II, n. 14), is the editor of the Gallimard edition of the *Cahiers* (I, Paris, 1973; II, 1974).

[11] Ibid., p. xxiii.

Biblical tonality of the text distances and mythologizes the internal conflict between ψ and φ, Angel and Eros, which remains nevertheless unresolved here as in *Faust*. But here, Elihu defends human love against the flaming Angel's admonitions, in one of Valéry's most beautiful apologies *pro vita,* for human happiness, against the "esprit pur" imaged as the Messenger of a Biblical, jealous god:

> A peine Elihu avec la fille de Chanaan eurent-ils achevé d'accomplir l'œuvre de chair et comme leurs yeux se rouvraient à la diversité des choses de la lumière, ils furent saisis d'une seule stupeur, car ils virent au pied de leur couche d'abomination, l'Ange dressé comme une flamme.
>
> Et sa Voix de glaive glacé leur dit jusqu'au fond de leurs cœurs, qui battaient la même épouvante: Qu'avez-vous fait? Et voici que vous avez mêlé vos corps d'iniquité, et échangé vos âmes et partagé une volupté comme des voleurs se partagent leur butin. Vous avez dérobé au Seigneur ce qu'il y avait en vous de puissance de feu, et l'avez sacrifié à cette œuvre de fornication, agissant l'un avec l'autre, chacun selon sa nature... Etc.

The last line indicates the fragmentary state of this text, "unfinished" like others about the warring halves of the Self, the human and the angelic, each jealously defending its own rights. The jealous Lord of Elihu — in the Bible Elihu is an interlocutor of Job (Job, XXXII) — did exist for Valéry, but as an inner ideal: "la plus grossière des hypothèses est de croire que Dieu existe objectivement...Oui! il existe et le Diable, mais en nous! ...En deux mots: Dieu est notre *idéal particulier.* Satan ce qui tend à nous en détourner" (*O*, II, 1431). Elihu is thus facing himself, his *moi angélique.* The text continues:

> —Mais Elihu, prenant la parole, lui répondit: Il est vrai, Monseigneur, mais puis-je te dire pourquoi nous le fîmes et quel est le sens de ce qui te paraît un sacrifice de péché? Nous savons que tu ne peux le comprendre et qu'il ne te fait pas besoin, car tu es le familier du feu de l'éternel! —Tu participes de Lui par ton essence, et tu brûles devant le Très Haut comme la roche de marbre au soleil devient splendide en elle-même, et se pénètre de sa force et la reflète de toutes parts, etc.

And the distance between the two, between light and darkness, remains insurmountable:

> Mais nous, formés de boue et si loin de la Lumière, en vérité, nous l'ignorons ... Et donc nous avons choisi le meilleur de nos instants de vie, et le plus doux et à la fois le plus ardent de nos actes, celui que nous désirons entre tous et qui a le privilège de créer— .... n'est-ce pas là le seuil de l'éternel, et quel autre moyen avons-nous de nous tirer de ce qui nous entoure et nous borne et de la terre et la vie qu'on y mène, assujettie?

"Mais nous," Lust had explained to that other spirit, the Devil, "nous portons nos clartés et nous portons nos ombres," but Elihu's Angel, *all* light and fire, does not understand that creature "formed of mud and so far from the Light:"

> L'Ange se dissipa, ces choses dites, comme se dissipe une conscience devant l'incompréhensible.

He brings to mind Valéry's last Angel, who "pendant une éternité, ..ne cessa de connaître et de ne pas comprendre" (*O,* I, 206).

Yet another mask of the angelic self is that of "le dernier Atlante," which a *Notebook* entry of 1943 links directly to the Angel: "je m'écarte de tous et j'exprime parfois ce sentiment très vif—en forme de plaisanterie en disant: Je suis le *dernier Atlante.* ...Je m'écarte de tous et me laisse dire (comme me le disait Degas) que je suis *Ange.* Et il y a du *vrai.* ...Eloignement—étonnement—recul" (*Cahiers,* XXVII, 475). This figure found its way into the œuvre in the posthumously published *Histoires brisées* in the prose sequence *L'Île de Xiphos,* whose first part is entitled "Le Dernier Atlante" (*O,* II, 436-50). "Xiphos," the Greek word for "sword," the sign of the Angel par excellence, links the angelic myth to that of the legendary island sunk beneath the ocean. The poet tells about that other world: "Ils l'appelaient XIPHOS, d'après eux le dernier fragment du monde qui a précédé celui-ci." And about its inhabitants:

> On en racontait mille merveilles (mais à voix basse), et telles que le plus important objet de l'esprit humain de maintenant serait (s'il existait des intelligences capable de s'y em-

ployer!) de démêler le vrai du faux dans ces légendes confidentielles, et de s'acharner à reconstituer le savoir, le pouvoir et les vouloirs des gens qui vécurent là.

Knowledge, power and will are preeminently angelic traits, and the inhabitants of the sunken island were, in fact, more angelic or divine than human: "on conte qu'ils en savaient mille fois mille fois plus que nous, ou toute autre chose, et c'est pourquoi je me demande si le nom d'Hommes leur convient? C'est à nous qu'ils le refuseraient sans doute, tandis que nous devrions peut-être les appeler *anges* ou *demi-dieux*" (*O*, II, 436).

The island of Xiphos was a sort of Eden where, in a deep, deep past "on avait les deux sexes, où science avec l'art n'étaient point séparés, ni la force ne l'était de la grâce, ni la liberté de la connaissance des lois, ni même le vice de la vertu," where, in fact, the world was not divided, where the Self was One, and where there was neither good nor evil. The wisest of our fallen world would be, "auprès de beaucoup de ces insulaires, des enfants comptant sur leurs doigts." And not merely the intelligences, but even the senses of these creatures of the lost Atlantis-Xiphos were much finer than those of man, for some of them "n'avaient jamais entendu deux sons identiques" (*O*, II, 437). Their severest punishment was banishment, that is to be expelled from Paradise. And their god was, indeed, superior to that of man: "il y avait à Xiphos un dieu qui rejetait les prières et jusqu'aux grimaces *intérieures* que d'autres dieux semblent exiger que les créatures leur fassent;" theirs was a god not of fearful creatures, but a paradoxical god of self-sufficient angels: "mais moi, ajoutait-il, je suis le dieu de ceux qui me résistent en tant que je suis, et qui me désirent en tant que je ne suis pas" (*O*, II, 440).

"Le Dernier Atlante" represents one of Valéry's last angelic figures, linked closely to the author himself: "je...me laisse dire (comme me le disait Degas), que je suis *Ange*." And the posthumously published Xiphos fragments are a final attempt to harmonize "être" and "connaître" poetically in the form of variations on the theme of the ancient myth. This late work remains, like the others on this fundamental theme, open-ended, another of the "Broken Stories," *Histoires brisées*.

CHAPTER VIII

"L'ANGE"

In May 1945, some two months before his death, Valéry completed his last poem, the prose poem "L'Ange" (*O*, I, 206-7). The great angel poem exists in numerous unpublished drafts which we have examined; [1] but during the more than twenty years that the text was maturing and becoming progressively more refined, its protagonist remained essentially the same: a solitary angelic Narcissus beholding his incomprehensible human reflection. This "last" Angel truly subsumes all of the intratextual angelic figures of the corpus of the *œuvre* which we have been discussing, so that in a sense the poem's deconstruction has preceded the presentation of its definitive text. We reproduce that text in its entirety:

L'ANGE

UNE *manière d'ange était assis sur le bord d'une fontaine. Il s'y mirait, et se voyait Homme, et en larmes, et il s'étonnait à l'extrême de s'apparaître dans l'onde nue cette proie d'une tristesse infinie.*

(Ou si l'on veut, il y avait une Tristesse en forme d'Homme qui ne se trouvait pas sa cause dans le ciel clair.)

La figure qui était sienne, la douleur qui s'y peignait, lui semblaient tout étrangères. Une apparence si misérable

---

[1] From the "premières études (Manuscrits et dactylographies 1921-1925)" to the three major "Révisions de 1945," preserved at the Bibliothèque Nationale (Dossier Paul Valéry "Ange"), which had their origin in the "L'Ange — (au bord) de la fontaine" of the 1921 Notebook (*Cahiers*, VIII, 370).

intéressait, exerçait, interrogeait en vain sa substance spi-
rituelle merveilleusement pure.

—"O mon Mal, *disait-il*; que m'êtes-vous?

Il essayait de se sourire; il se pleurait. Cette infidélité
de son visage confondait son intelligence parfaite; et cet air
si particulier qu'il observait, une affection si accidentelle de
ses traits, leur expression tellement inégale à l'universalité
de sa connaissance limpide, en blessaient mystérieusement
l'unité.

—"Je n'ai pas sujet de pleurer, *disait-il*, et même, je ne
puis en avoir".

Le Mouvement de sa Raison dans sa lumière d'éternelle
attente, trouvait une question inconnue suspendre son opé-
ration infaillible, car ce qui cause la douleur dans nos natu-
res inexactes ne fait naître qu'une question chez les essences
absolues;—cependant que, pour nous, toute question est ou
sera douleur.

—"Qui donc est celui-ci qui s'aime tant qu'il se tourmente? *disait-il*. Je comprends toute chose; et pourtant, je
vois bien que je souffre. Ce visage est bien mon visage; ces
pleurs, mes pleurs... Et pourtant, ne suis-je pas cette puissance de transparence de qui ce visage et ces pleurs, et leur
cause, et ce qui dissiperait cette cause, ne sont que d'imper-
ceptibles grains de durée?

Mais ces pensées avaient beau se produire et propager
dans toute la plénitude de la sphère de la pensée, les simi-
litudes se répondre, les contrastes se déclarer et se résoudre,
et le miracle de la clarté incessament s'accomplir, et toutes
les Idées étinceler à la lueur de chacune d'entre elles, comme
les joyaux qu'elles sont de la couronne de la connaissance
unitive, rien toutefois qui fût de l'espèce d'un mal ne parais-
sait à son regard sans défaut, rien par quoi s'expliquât ce
visage de détresse et ces larmes qu'il lui voyait à travers les
larmes.

—"Ce que je suis de pur, *disait-il*, Intelligence qui
consume sans effort toute chose créée, sans qu'aucune en
retour ne l'affecte ni ne l'altère, ne peut point se reconnaître
dans ce visage porteur de pleurs, dans ces yeux dont la lumière qui les compose est comme attendrie par l'humide
imminence de leurs larmes."

—Et comment se peut-il que pâtisse à ce point ce bel
éploré qui est à moi, et qui est de moi, puisqu'enfin je vois
tout ce qu'il est, car je suis connaissance de toute chose, et
que l'on ne peut soufrir que pour en ignorer quelqu'une?

"O mon étonnement, *disait-il,* Tête charmante et triste,
il y a donc autre chose que la lumière?"

Et il s'interrogeait dans l'univers de sa substance spi-
rituelle merveilleusement pure, où toutes les idées vivaient
également distantes entre elles et de lui-même, et dans une
telle perfection de leur harmonie et promptitude de leurs
correspondances, qu'on eût dit qu'il eût pu s'évanouir, et le
système, étincelant comme un diadème, de leur nécessité
simultanée subsister par soi seul dans sa sublime plénitude.

Et pendant une éternité, il ne cessa de connaître et de
ne pas comprendre.

Mai 1945.

Valéry's last, broken Angel appears, then, in a prose poem, itself
a kind of "broken genre" in the sense that it came into its own
during a period characterized by the break-up or dissolution of
some of the established and traditional forms of literary expression,
and is symptomatic or representative of that break-up. It is cus-
tomarily defined, moreover, by negations, i.e., by defining what it is
not and how it differs from the forms from which it broke away. [2]
And as Barbara Johnson has shown in her reading of Baudelaire and
Mallarmé, the "poème en prose" signals a crisis not merely in poetry,
but in prose as well. [3]

The most obvious formal aspects of the text, like the title that
sets if off, and the date constituting its closure, confer on it the

---

[2] Thus, e.g., in the *Princeton Encyclopedia of Poetry and Poetics* (Princeton: 1974), p. 664: "A composition able to have any or all features of the
lyric, except that it is put on the page — though not conceived of — as prose.
It differs from poetic prose in that it is short and compact, from free verse in
that it has no line breaks, from a short prose passage in that it has, usually,
more pronounced rhythm, sonorous effects, imagery, and density of expression.
It may contain even inner rhyme and metrical runs. Its length, generally, is
from half a page (one or two paragraphs) to three or four pages, i.e., that of
the average lyrical poem..."

[3] Barbara Johnson, *Défigurations du langage poétique* (Paris: Flammarion,
1979), pp. 161 ff.

appearance of a self-contained unit of discourse, the "short, over-determined, and clearcut unit of significance," which empirically defines the genre whose semiotics has recently been analyzed by Michael Riffaterre.[4] According to this semiotics of the prose poem (the first systematic one to our knowledge), our text's matrix, which bears and generates its significance, is the title, a "loaded" term indeed in Valéry's poetic universe. Our prose poem falls into Riffaterre's second category, "characterized by *one derivation representing the subject of the matrix sentence and one its predicate*," the two being "opposed to each other by semantic incompatibility." Here it is, of course, the Angel — "this power of transparency," "Intelligence that consumes without effort every created thing, without any in return affecting or altering it," "knowledge of all things" — who is *seated* by the fountain that reflects him as Man!, "a Sorrow in the form of Man," "this prey to an infinite sorrow," "so miserable an appearance." Here is a double incompatibility: the abstract and immaterial takes on concrete and material form (Angel seated), and a "transparency" produces its reflection! The text could, in fact, serve as an *exemplum* of that category of prose poems, in which "oppositions within grammatically compatible sequences create antinomies that cancel visualization and verisimilitude." Again conforming to Riffaterre's semiological schema, the poem offers a quandary, and "this quandary is also the key to the significance of the text as a whole." For it is constructed of that very opposition, that contradiction in terms — "Ange-Homme" — which it develops without resolving, thereby reflecting all the Angel texts of the corpus, of which it also remains, though a poem in and for itself, an open-ended fragment.

The other most obvious formal aspect of the text, besides title and closure, is its graphic division into italicized and non-italicized paragraphs, dividing it into descriptive and direct discourse. This division accentuates a fundamental dichotomy of the poem, its two personae: that of the discoursing Angel, its subject on the one hand, and that of the scriptor who describes him as the object of his own vision and discourse on the other. From the beginning, then, the

[4] Michael Riffaterre, *Semiotics of Poetry* (Bloomington: Indiana University Press, 1978), pp. 116-24.

Angel is defeated here not merely in seeing himself betrayed by his mirror image, but, ironically, in being *seen,* in being an object for another observer. Only the first conflict is revealed by a cursory referential reading; the other is rhetorically disguised so that the implied reader of the poem suspends disbelief and accepts the poetic fiction of the solitary Narcissus-Angel, overlooking that within the text the Angel is presented as the creature of an omniscient author-maker who not merely de-scribes him, but reads — and writes — the very thoughts of the creature he has, after all, formed after his own (self-)image. In this connection, we must recall Teste, who would reduce the world to an object without being object for another, in the theatre observing "the others," that is the audience for whom he is invisible, as he is surprised by the glance of his interlocutor, the first-person- or *ego-scriptor* of that text. Within the context of Valéryan angelology, of which our Narcissus-Angel represents the culmination, he should suffer an "ange-Lionardo's" "luminous torture," that is "that one sees everything, without ceasing to feel that one is still *visible,* and the conceivable object of a foreign attention." What the rhetorical mystification, legitimate in a poetic text, hides is that the angelic Narcissus is betrayed not merely by what he sees, but by his own visibility, that is by the very poem that images him. And we are reminded of one of Valéry's great demystifiers, former Angel himself, demonstrating — in person — that God's Fall was Creation!

The poem's first paragraph has remained practically unchanged from the 1921-22 manuscript versions. But in the earliest draft, in which this section is not yet italicized, Valéry did underline two words: "homme" and "apparaître," as, in that draft, he also underscored the word "apparence" in what is now the third paragraph. These graphic emphases accentuate, of course, the fundamental contradiction which we just pointed out: that of the Angel's *appearance,* which is linked to his *human* nature, the Narcissus. In the version of *Cahier* VIII (1921-22), only "homme" is underlined. This obvious conflict of "Ange" and "Narcisse" is much more thoroughly disguised in the definitive text. In all versions, however, the Angel is a Narcissus confronting his mirror image in the fountain. And what he sees is a face in tears, which in the poem signals the confrontation of intellect and affect, or emotion in its physical manifestation.

That tears should play a prominent part in the poet's last composition should not surprise us; not merely is the motif of "la larme" intimately linked to this poem's theme, a visible sign of the Angel's sorrow, but it is fundamental throughout Valéry's poetic universe, taken up repeatedly in both verse and prose. The poet had devoted an entire lyric paragraph of his major poem, "La Jeune Parque," to its exploration:

> Larme qui fais trembler à mes regards humains
> Une variété de funèbres chemins;
> Tu procèdes de l'âme, orgueil du labyrinthe.
> . . . .
> D'où nais-tu? Quel travail toujours triste et nouveau
> Te tire avec retard, Larme, de l'ombre amère? (O, I, 104)

Here, too, the tear is immediately associated with the human, "my mortal glance"; and its provenance remains mysterious. The obscure and "bitter shade" in which it originates is precisely that unfathomable human depth which our all-knowing Angel is unable to comprehend.

The Angel's "extreme astonishment" at seeing tears in his image, and the questions subsequent to that surprise, reflect Valéry's lifelong preoccupation with the inexplicable phenomenon. For example, this Notebook entry of the thirties (*Cahiers*, XVII, 693) again stresses both the intimate and hidden relationship of tears and the body, and also the incomprehensibility of tears to the mind:

> —Une larme qui vient de ton sang au moment de ta peine et qui coule sur ton visage, ignorante du prix payé, étonnant l'esprit qui ne peut concevoir la cause et la génération de cette transmutation. Car le propre de l'esprit est d'ignorer de la vie tout ce qui lui semble inutile à son opération.

Is the prose poem not a mytho-poetization of this text?

In an entry of a 1910 *Notebook* (*Cahiers*, IV, 587), Valéry associates tears with a voice, probably his mother's: "à un certain âge tendre, j'ai peut-être entendu une voix, un contr'alto profondément émouvant . . . . Une voix qui touche aux larmes..." Here tears are associated with the poet's most profoundly human origins; and we have explored elsewhere the tears that come, again inexplicably, at dawn, the moment of the *Moi pur* par excellence.

In the "Eros" section of a *Notebook* contemporary with the early drafts of the "Ange" (*Cahiers,* VIII, 310), the poet images the obscure region of tears as an almost oneirically-oppressive grotto that the Self crosses only to arrive at the threshold of the unanswerable: "...Traversée, dans l'obscurité affreuse, la grotte des Larmes, on se trouve sous des arches énormes bizarrement disposées qui se pénètrent, s'intersectent étrangement. C'est le porche dit 'des Grandes Questions.' " Here, as in "L'Ange," the enigma of tears and their mysterious origin remains unsolved. Five of the Angel's seven utterances are questions; rhetorical questions that appeal to no one for an answer. We finally cite one more "Eros" passage (*Cahiers,* XVI, 202) on tears, in which Love is featured as a combat against intelligence leading to Despair and to a Region close to tears. The passage is related to the Angel-nexus particularly in its Faustian development; it accentuates the divided being of a Narcissus-Angel, and the mind's exasperation with nature's cyclical returns, which we have already discussed at length:

> Le combat d'Amour contre l'intelligence à haute puissance—Toute une mythologie— ...Division de l'être. Le point capital est la puissance cyclique, de *répétition* créée et exaspérée par obstacles,—en lutte atroce avec la défense de l'Esprit, duquel l'essence est non-répétition. ...Désespoir —Région aux bords de larmes—

In "L'Ange," the tears of the Angel and Narcissus are intimately linked to the image of water, the *Urelement* of Life itself, which is the Angel's mirror, "l'onde nue" that reflects him. In the early drafts, the Angel is reflected merely "dans l'onde," changed in one of the 1945 versions to "l'onde vide; " but the final synecdoche and its personification with "naked" stresses the femininity of the water — sole support of the Angel's image. This was likewise stressed in the "Fragments du Narcisse," where the water is mythologized into the traditional Nymphs, and where the spring's personifications all evoke feminine attributes: "l'onde mystérieuse: Nymphes! ," "belles fontaines," "Fontaine, ma fontaine ..Sœur tranquille du Sort!," "O présence pensive, eau calme," "mon onde sage, infidèle et la même." And the maternal, rhythmic and cyclical nature of water, reflecting the element's interdependence with the planet's life, is frequently stressed in Valéry's verse and prose. We recall "La mer,

la mer, toujours recommencée" (O, I, 147) of "Le Cimetière marin,"
where, as in "L'Ange," a water-light (matter-spirit) polarity is created; and again, the prose poem "Louanges de l'eau" [my emphasis],
in which the poet asks: "Combien cependant conçoivent que la VIE
n'est guère que l'eau organisée?" (O, I, 203). And the free verse
poem "Comme au Bord de la mer" is entirely structured on the
rhythmic "transformation monotone/De l'eau en eau" (Cahiers, IV,
671). The feminine water, das Weibliche, supports the Angel's image
and reflects his tears.

From "L'Ange's" first versions, the Angel is the "proie d'une
tristesse infinie," the 1921 version showing "douleur" in place of
"tristesse," the latter written over it as an alternate. In one draft
"cette proie" is replaced by "l'objet," but the poet chooses "prey"
in all the other versions, a metaphor surely intended to stress that
the Angel is himself a victim, and also to allude distantly to his
creaturely nature — his predicament of an animal hunted down by a
predator for food. He is consumed by the "infinite sadness/sorrow"
associated with the Angel from his first appearance in this poetic
universe. The appearance of the golden Angel "arising at the harsh
threshold of the sepulchre" of the 1891 letter to Gide was preceded
by a "sadness not of this world:" "Ma tristesse n'est pas de ce
monde. Au seuil rude du sépulcre surgit un ange d'or." In the 1921
version of "L'Ange," the sadness/sorrow simultaneously is and is
not his, like the mirror image in which the Angel sees himself: "en
proie à une $\frac{\text{tristesse}}{\text{douleur}}$ infinie - sa douleur lui semblait à la fois aussi
étrangère à lui-même et aussi attachée à lui-même que ce visage de
quelqu'un qui se voit dans une glace lui paraît changé étranger et
cependant sien." And in the "A B C" sequence, contemporary with
this version, we found the angelic, but divided, Self again the victim
of sadness: "son âme...ange fait de lumière, se recueille, s'attriste, et
s'enfuit..." Finally, in "Paraboles" of the poet's late period, Man
appeared under the sign of Sorrow in the Garden, "une souffrance
sans pareille" that separates him from both Angel and beasts and
that ruffles the smooth surface of the mirror reflecting him.

Sadness is likewise the attribute of Narcissus, his inherent characteristic; in "Narcisse parle," he languishes for his "sad beauty,"
"ma triste beauté" and adores his "uncertain/Flesh blossoming
sadly for the solitude," "l'incertaine/Chair pour la solitude éclose

tristement" (*O*, I, 82, 83). And the entire poetic tonality of the
"Fragments du Narcisse" is that of a haunting sadness; Narcissus'
beauty is sad, as is his glance, as is the water reflecting him: "ma
beauté, ma douleur," "mes tristes regards," "l'eau triste."

The following paragraph of "L'Ange," a variation on the "tristesse" motif, developed only gradually in the poet's creative imagination; it is absent from the earliest drafts, and in two later ones
the phrase "dans le ciel clair," one variant of which reads "dans (ce)
ciel (pur)," was "dans un Ange." The hesitations suggest the equiv-
alency of "Angel" and the "clear (pure) sky," all of them developing
another polarity of the text, that of Angel-altitude (in its sense of
height) and that of Man-depth, both in their literal and figurative
intentions. We recall Sémiramis' soaring angelic aspiration — fun-
damentally linked to the Angel archetype — "Altitude, mon Altitude, mon Ciel; " and the celebration of the water's unfathomable
depth in the "Fragments du Narcisse," the maternal fountain "Claire,
mais si profonde; " and the famous "Œil qui gardes en toi/Tant
de sommeil sous un voile de flamme" of the "Cimetière marin." In
"L'Ange," the impersonal pronoun and the phrase "si l'on veut"
distance the image introduced, while "a Sorrow in the form of
Man" reifies both the form and the feeling, a movement continued
in the following section, which we find with very minor variants in
most of the anterior drafts.

At this point in the poem, the reflected "figure" seems almost
coincidentally that of the Angel — observer himself; the poet stresses its remoteness, its utter *externality* to the angel, who *sees* the
"suffering painted on it," and to whom it seems "all strange (foreign)." The "figure" seems to the Angel not even born, its pain not
really suffered; they appear to be not really part of him whom they
"interest" and fascinate like an object-phenomenon outside of himself: "so miserable an appearance! " But this, as we have seen, is
profoundly characteristic of the Narcissus-Angel's very essence: the
inner split — here externalized — in which one part of the Self
beholds the other, a split which, we recall, gave birth to both the
Valéryan Angel and to his Narcissus. From the beginning, we found
the two figures linked, but their ultimate and explicit fusion is
achieved in "L'Ange": the Angel-Narcissus' two selves divided by
a mirror. And this "dédoublement intérieur" — an inversion of

Mallarmé's "Je me mire et me vois ange!," [5] a consecration — is the Fall from innocence. Thus, from the beginning also, Valéry's is a fallen Angel. The "marvelously pure spiritual substance" and its "suffering" and "so miserable an appearance" suggest the distance of our earth from its Eden.

And then the Angel speaks. This signals yet another split, or break, *within* the "marvelously pure spiritual substance" itself, as well as a falling *away* from the origin. For in assuming language, the Angel sacrifices his uniqueness — his position as a species to himself — in thinking-speaking by and through a medium shared with the others, even if they are of his kind. Nietzsche and Freud, and the Structuralists after them, have shown us that the "subject" is but the instrument through and by which those forces which more or less control it express themselves. Narcissus' fragile figure in the fountain, threatened by night and death, is the "subject's" poetic image. The Angel becomes, moreover, divided into a "bouche-oreille," Valéry's term for the inner division fundamental to speech and thought, whether one thinks, or speaks, to oneself or to the other(s). At the root of all thought, as Valéry repeatedly explains in the Notebooks, is that *dédoublement* which alone makes it possible. In an entry entitled "Division de l'être," he states:

> La pensée exige une division interne—et que le même puisse s'opposer au même—déguisant la même énergie en plusieurs personnes. Il faut trouver en soi *celui* qui ne sait pas et *celui* qui sait, *celui* qui attend et *celui* qui vient, *celui* qui propose et *celui* qui objecte, celui qui cherche et celui qui trouve ou donne . . . . Cette divisibilité se trouve également dans la sensation du *temps*. Le temps exige la division de l'être. Et de même la division φ ψ. Ce sont pôles. (*Cahiers,* XV, 723)

The Angel has fallen simultaneously into time and speech that render him human, a Narcissus-Angel. Narcissus, we recall, *speaks,* not merely in the "Narcisse parle"; the "Fragments du Narcisse" consist, too, entirely of the protagonist's discourse, directed at times to the fountain, his mirror, to himself and his mirror image, and finally to the gods.

---

[5] Mallarmé, *Œuvres,* p. 33.

The paradox of the Angel *speaking* probabably escapes the poem's implied reader who has already accepted the Angel *seated* by the fountain. He merely hears the Angel's words: "Oh my pain, what are you to me?" His pain, however, is precisely to have fallen — into space and time. This is the Angel's "Mal" and cause of his tears: his humanity. Thus we must not confuse the Angel's "mal" with the traditionally moralistic "Good and Evil," which were not Valéry's — nor his Angel's — concern. In one of the "Ego" passages of the *Notebooks,* in which, as so frequently, he sets himself apart from his friend Gide and Gidean "moralisme," Valéry explains the difference, linking his own stance, again, to the angelic:

> Du *Journal* d'André. Je ne conçois pas ce genre peccamineux d'esprit. Moralisme et immoralisme, me paraissent choses aussi ennuyeuses l'une que l'autre. Le Bien et le Mal doivent se faire inconsciemment. J'appelle *Ange,* celui qui porte la Lumière. Il est vrai que ce nom est mal sonnant. Mais la Lumière est la Lumière. *Le Bien et le Mal ne supportent pas la réflexion* qui les renvoie 1° au siècle; 2° à la sensibilité particulière [a marginal note here reads: "Faust III"]. (*Cahiers,* XXVI, 378)

Valéry's Angel — need we recall? — is secularized, as is his "Mal."

"Il essayait de se sourire: il se pleurait," continues the text. But the Angel did not, in fact, smile to himself, but rather at his mirror image, which wept. Had he remained self-contained, smiled to himself rather than at the image in the fountain, he would never have seen the tears. One of the earliest drafts stresses the Angel's fascination with his image: "Mais il ne pouvait pas se détacher de son regard;" and in the *Cahier* VIII version, the division between the beholder and the one beheld (we are not speaking here of the narrator who describes the Angel!) is also more accentuated: "il essayait de se sourire. Il se pleurait. Qui es-tu se disait-il tout bas. Et plus bas redisait-il: Qui est moi celui-ci qui tant se tourmente, ou celui-là qui le regarde? Suis-je celui qui peut détourner les yeux ou celui qui ne peut être vu sans que la douleur soit?" The "one who cannot be seen without sorrow," we recall from "Paraboles," is Man: "MAN was that event: / . . . . I knew it by a pain without equal. / . . . A knowledge of suffering, a suffering of knowledge." Part of the *Cahier* VIII draft was incorporated into the Angel's third speech of the definitive text. Again, the Angel's betrayal is not merely the "false" mirror image, the appearance that lies, but the existence of any image whatsoever, that "son intelligence parfaite" should have a "visage." The Angel's unity was destroyed not by the "accidental affection of his features, their expression unequal to the universality of his clear knowledge," but by the very fact of being "featured" at all. This, the poem insists, "wounded [the] mysterious unity" of "his perfect intelligence," or "the universality of his clear knowledge." The Angel's wholeness, or unity, is broken by his splitting in two: Angel-Narcissus, Narcissus-Angel. And the text continues to modulate precisely this polarity: weeping Narcissus-impassible Angel, or the un-imageable "perfect intelligence," the "universality of his clear knowledge" and the image of human suffering. This "semantic incompatibility," we noted, constitutes stress-lines supporting the entire textual construct.

Throughout the poem, it is the Angel-Narcissus' beholder, the voice of the de-scriptive text, who not merely describes but explains the paradox, an oxymoron almost, inherent in the figure he objectifies, while the Angel fails to understand his Fall. We recall the Angel "Ghimmel" of the "L'Ange et l'amour" dossier, and his incomprehension as he feels himself become "humanized:" "L'Ange à la fontaine/L'ange Ghimmel se sent humaniser - /il ne comprend pas ce qui lui survient."

The narrator-beholder's voice, however, identifies itself with "us," mankind, the implied reader, as in the following paragraph, where, after the Angel has again questioned and rejected the weeping of his image, he refers to "our inexact natures" in contrast to that of the Angels, their "absolute essences." This section developed only gradually; absent from the first drafts, it slowly takes on form in subsequent versions, to its final perfection in rhythm and balance in the definitive text. Entirely made up of abstractions and thus lacking the referential support of imagery, it rests exclusively on its rhetorical and poetic strength and beauty: "The Movement of his Reason" is harmoniously balanced by "the light of eternal expectation," and "its infallible operation" then held in equipoise, or equilibrium, "suspended by un unknown question." This is the Angelic, a harmonious realm of pure form and correspondences, of a self-sufficient, or non-referential, "système," to which the text will return later, in the closing section. In contrast to the angelic, the human, "our" domain, introduced by "car," that coordinate conjunction which always announces ex-planation, proof and reasons, is represented by a choppy phrase of one-syllable words, "car ce qui cause." This phrase leads to "la douleur" in "*our* inexact natures," contrasted with "the absolute essences." In the human, intellectual vision yields to the emotions. What is question for the angels, is sorrow for us; and yet, again, the two natures will be fused in the Angelic Narcissus, the Narcissistic Angel, who asks himself, "Who loves himself so much that he torments himself?" The answer is in the "Fragments du Narcisse:" it is Narcissus, "cette parfaite proie,/Du monstre de s'aimer." The Angel who "understand[s] all things," significantly "see[s] that I [he] suffer[s]." Not "I suffer," but "I *see* that I do." Were he not a Narcissus, tied to his image, he would not know tears or suffering. "This power of transparency" could not project an image or a shadow, thus could not reflect or even refract light, for it should be that pure crystal of lucidity which, in one of the fragments of the "Teste" cycle we saw culminate in "L'Homme de verre."

A variant of this angelic "Homme de verre" is the "tête—Teste?—réfringente," the "refrigent head," of a 1940 *Notebook* entry. The entry covers a full page, the lines much more widely spaced than usual, with only one word crossed out. It flows:

> J'aurais voulu te vouer à former le cristal de chaque chose, ma Tête — et que tu divises le désordre que présente l'espace et que développe le temps, pour en tirer les puretés qui te fassent ton monde propre, de manière que ta lumière dans cette structure réfringente revienne et se forme sur elle-même dans l'instant, substituant à l'espace l'ordre et au temps une éternité. Et ainsi je serais sans être et je ne serais pas sans ne pas être—et la mort n'étant qu'un effet du monde naturel, comme la vie; toutes deux inséparables de lui, il arriverait que le décomposant et le résolvant de la sorte, et la vie avec lui la mort s'évanouirait avec elle et avec lui. (*Cahiers,* XXIV, 3)

Here the scriptor, the persona, of the text identifies with the angelic which is raised beyond both space and time into "another world," "your own world," which must be that of the Angel, pure Nothingness that dissolves both life and death. In contrast to this timeless lucidity, are not Narcissus' face of sorrow, "et ces pleurs, et leur cause," mere "imperceptible grains of duration?" Human sorrow, then, is a speck, hardly discernable, when set against the Angel's eternity, like the foam of the sea against its eternal cause: "Quel pur travail de fins éclairs consume/Maint diamant d'imperceptible écume,/ .... Ouvrages purs d'une éternelle cause." All the verbs of the "tête réfringente" text, significantly, are in the conditional or subjunctive moods, as they graph, or trace, an aspiration. But our Angel sits by the fountain: "this face is indeed my face; these tears, my tears..."

The following paragraph of "L'Ange," a crescendo in the elaboration of the angelic theme, develops very gradually from weak origins in the October 1921 version, to reach its final, accomplished form in the published poem. Throughout successive drafts, its composer is struggling with the rhythm of the phrases as well as with some of the key figures, such as "la sphère de la pensée" and "la couronne de la connaissance unitive," which are not yet crystalized even as late as the 1945 drafts. The beauty of the section, then, grew slowly out of labor over the years and did not come to perfection until the very end of the poet's life. It thus constitutes a kind of culmination, the very "aboutissement" and fulfillment that the text in fact traces, in vain: "But in vain were these thoughts produced and propagated in all fullness..."

The highly charged sentence-paragraph opens with multiple alliteration and internal rhyme, sustained in balance, with ten syllables each in the two rhythmic runs: "Mais ces pensées avaient beau se produire/et/propager dans toute la plénitude." These lead into the key symbolic figure of "la sphère de la pensée," which supports an accumulation of infinitive phrases accentuating the impersonal, the super- and supra-human nature of the operations of the angelic mind/spirit: "les similitudes se répondre," "les contrastes se déclarer et se résoudre," "le miracle de la clarté incessamment s'accomplir," "toutes les Idées étinceler...." The "Ideas sparkling at the gleam of each one of them" compose the "jewels" of "the crown of unitive knowledge," variant and development of "the sphere of thought" mentioned above, and a figure for that impersonal "system" of pure thought which in the poem's closing becomes the Angel's sparkling diadem, "le système étincelant comme un diadème." It is the poetic development of the ideal of the "Tête réfringente"; in the "Cimetière marin," we encountered it as the sun's — the source of all light's—"Tête complète et parfait diadème." And in the "Agathe" sequence of *Teste,* we recall, there was yet another variant of that obsessive thematic image.

All the operations of the angelic mind, the "sphere of thought," are, significantly, poetic ones. That mind concerns itself with "corresponding similitudes" which are certainly rhymes, as in "Aurore" where the awakening poet addresses his "Similitudes amies/Qui brillez parmi les mots"! (*O,* I, 111); with the "contrasts declaring and resolving themselves" that evoke the play of multiple polarities characteristic of so much of Valéry's poetry; with the "miracle of clarity accomplished" regularly in even the most seductive of his verse; with, finally, the "sparkling Ideas," or thoughts that Valéry elsewhere likens to the hidden nutritive virtue of the pure delight of poetry: "La pensée doit être cachée dans les vers comme la vertu nutritive dans un fruit. Un fruit est nourriture, mais il ne paraît que délice. On ne perçoit que du plaisir, mais on reçoit une substance" (*O,* II, 547-8). As we observed in connection with another of Valéry's fallen angels, the Narcissus-Angel, too, is a poet.

In "L'Ange," the "couronne de la connaissance unitive" supports the ideal of unity to which the divided Angel aspires, by the image of the "crown," as the image of the "sphere" had done earlier in the poem. It refers us back to the poem's fifth section which closed on the Angel's "unité," that was "mysteriously wounded" by his division into observer and image, "Ange" and "Narcisse." "L'unité" was there grounded in "l'universalité de sa connaissance limpide," a limpidity or clarity clouded, however, by tears. The ideal figured by the symbolic image of the crown of thought haunted the poet; we found it earlier in "La Jeune Parque": her "pensive crown," "La pensive couronne échappe à mes esprits." The fragments of the Angel are, as we have tried to demonstrate, scattered everywhere throughout the Valéryan poetic universe.

After the movement's culmination with "la couronne de la connaissance unitive," comes the "falling off," from the unity and harmony to which the Angel aspires, into division and dissonance. And this break is again marked by a contrast in language, by choppy phrasing reinforced with unpoetic expressions like the adverb "toutefois" and the logos of logic, "rien toutefois qui fût de l'espèce d'un mal." The harsh, unsonorous and negative phrase is then almost echoed by the repetition of the "rien" which opened the break: "rien par quoi s'expliquât..." We have already touched on the nature of the Angel's "mal"; it escapes his "faultless gaze," for its essence is absence, absence of the angelic, just as Evil is sometimes defined in the patristic tradition as the Absence of the Divine, or a lacuna in Being. In his penultimate question, the Angel says that he sees "all that he is," since he is "knowledge of all things," and that he can "suffer only from not knowing." Seeing "the beautiful weeping one," the Angel's "faultless gaze" fails to see and know what his maker — the poem's other voice that has established its complicity with us, the readers — describes: Narcissus, a fallen Angel, Narcissus, the very image of the loss of unity, the Self divided by a mirror into "I" and "My-Self," a fleeting self and its fragile reflection. Knowledge, we recall, will come after the Fall — we understand more than do the Angels and the Beasts.

We have mentioned that the early drafts stress the Angel's fascination with his inexplicable image, from which he cannot tear himself away: "Il ne pouvait pas se dérober à cette vue, comme il ne pouvait se défendre..." "Ce que je suis de pur, *disait-il,* Intelligence..." had read, in one of the anterior (1921) versions, significantly, "ce que j'ai d'invisible, disait-il, et qui est maître." As late as a 1945 draft, we still read "invisible" for "pure"; in most of these anterior versions the Angel's invisibility is accentuated, underlining the paradox of his reflection, his image in the fountain. Our Angel's purity, his "intelligence that consumes without effort all created things, without their affecting or altering it in return" equates the angelic essence with fire, the *ignis sunt* Valéry took over from the angelology of the tradition; we recall: "...la *Nature Angélique*— Qu'entends-tu par ces mots? Ce qui est *pur en soi*—qui touche à tout, et n'est par rien touché... ce qui refuse d'avoir été—ce qui veut tout consumer—Ignis sunt. 'L'acte pur' des scholastiques"; and that comment had its reverberations throughout the *œuvre*. In fact, Valéry's very first Angel had eyes of flame—"et me montre la flamme de ses yeux—ses yeux qui ont vu le songe du Très Pur"; and the Seraphim [saraph, to burn] of the early "Le Jeune Prêtre" were "wearing strange fires"; finally, Sémiramis, the angelic mythic

figure of the poet's maturity, is ultimately consumed by and assumed
into the sun in a blazing ascension. Valéry's angels are made of fire,
hence diametrically opposed to Narcissus' water-borne image. This
polarity is reflected, literally and microcosmically as it were, in our
Angel's very eyes: "dans ces yeux dont *la lumière qui les compose
est comme attendrie par l'humide imminence de leurs larmes.*"

The phrase "Et comment se peut-il que pâtisse à ce point ce bel
éploré" read in the third 1945 revision: "Et comment se peut-il que
je pâtisse à ce point ce bel éploré." The change expresses a shift in
meaning centering on the basic problem of identity with and estran-
gement from the other (self), the alienation and distance being
accentuated by the omission of "je" in the definitive version. In both
versions, however, the text continues "who is mine, and who is of
me," establishing the Angel's new self-knowledge, his awakening
recognition of Narcissus as his (him-)self. "Ce bel éploré," and sad
beauty, beautiful sadness, is Narcissus from his initial appearance
in Valéry's *œuvre*; in "Narcisse parle," he pines for his sad beauty:
"Je languis de beauté/.... Je languis, ô saphir, par ma triste beauté! "; in the "Fragments," he entreats the water: "Sans vous, belles
fontaines,/Ma beauté, ma douleur, me seraient incertaines." And in
the "Cantate du Narcisse" of the poet's later years (1939), his very
beauty, as in the Ovidian myth, is Narcissus' curse: "Votre seule
beauté ne vous promet que pleurs" (*O*, I, 409). But in the "Cantate
du Narcisse," Narcissus, in his pride — angelic trait par excellence —
calls on the Sun in a passage that recalls Sémiramis, and in which he
becomes "angelic" in the Valéryan sense:

> Soleil... Seul avec toi, seul comme Toi, Soleil
> Toi dont l'orgueil s'accorde à mon secret conseil;
> Toi qui dans les chemins de la pleine altitude
> Jamais ne trouves ton pareil,
> Souffre entre nos destins quelque similitude. (*O*, I, 406)

Then Narcissus goes on to liken his "eternal returns" to the fountain
to those of the sun which make his own image possible. This latest
of Valéryan Narcissi is, in his identification with the Sun, an Angelic
Narcissus revealing his kinship with our Narcissistic Angel.

We return to "L'Ange": Narcissus' is the "charming and sad"
face, but the astonishment and the question ("is there then something

other than light?") are the Angel's. In the poem's earliest extant draft, "astonishment" was significantly "distance," and the "charming head" identified with the Angel's "mal"; the division between angel and image was accentuated, and the angelic self identified with the sun: "O mon éloignement,... tête charmante, qui êtes vous et Mal... ô mon mal, que m'êtes-vous? Vous êtes vrais et je suis vrai. Mais vous l'êtes amèrement et moi comme le soleil." In another draft of 1921, the Angel's last question, "il y a donc autre chose que la lumière?" reads "Il y a donc quelque autre *chose* que la misère," the segment not placed in final position, nor marked as a question. The utterance of the definitive version, then, echoes the earlier one, despite the total opposition of the key word; "lumière" and "misère" are antonyms within this poetic universe. The substitution suggests a shift in point of view: the question of the definitive version is posed by the angelic self, that of the draft by the human one; the angel knows only light and is astonished at human opacity, while man (we recall "Paraboles") knows only pain and is astonished at light and transparency. Purely as poetry, both phrases are equally polished; it is their referential value that carries the opposition, a reversal of inner points of view. Fittingly, however, the last word of the Angel's last utterance — a question — is "lumière," for "J'appelle *Ange,* celui qui porte la Lumière...la Lumière est la Lumière."

But in "L'Ange," the Angel does not have the last word. That belongs to his maker's persona, who once more conjures up the miraculous: the poetic mirage of the angelic mind, the "marvelously pure spiritual substance," whose life consists of ideas without external object, each idea distinct, yet all synchronized in a timeless, simultaneous harmony of perfect correspondences. It is that uncontaminated pure construct of an angelic mind which should ideally subsist even without the Angel: a "sparkling diadem" worn by no one. This angelic "crown" or "sphere of thought" is the culminating elaboration of an ideal symbolic image for the "esprit pur" that haunts the œuvre. The "Zéro mathématique" is its less poetic figure; and its origins, in fact, lie in Valéry's early dream of the *Arithmetica Universalis,* his flirtation with mathematics, a pure, self-contained "a priori" system "des *constructions* comme on dit en géométrie." But ideally this system or logic would be one of its kind, as is each

Angel. When the dream of the arithmetical or geometrical system was left behind, the ideal subsisted, henceforth to be "poetized." Its earliest poetic elaboration appeared in "Agathe." At the culmination of her nocturnal voyage of the mind, as Agathe approached its pure "Zéro," a virtual system independent or void of all "content," Agathe-Teste had reached the Absolute of the Angel:

> L'ensemble de connaissances diverses, également imminentes, qui me constitue, ...forme maintenant un système nul ou indifférent à ce qu'il vient de produire ou approfondir, quand l'ombre imaginaire doucement cède à toute naissance, et c'est l'esprit.

In one of the 1945 drafts of "L'Ange," the ideas are compared to stars, a beautiful simile suggesting different astronomical points that together constitute a single harmonious, luminous system; a simile that could be applied to the angelic fragments in Valéry's poetic universe as well:

> Et il s'interrogeait dans l'univers de sa connaissance où toutes les idées se voyaient également distantes de lui, et semblaient mystérieusement se répondre et se regarder comme des astres, à ce point de perfection dans leur correspondances qu'on eût dit qu'il eût pu s'évanouir, et elles subsister comme un système qui existe par soi-même.

But the human mind, on the contrary, cannot subsist without a human existence to support it, and in that human mind there are no thoughts that are not thoughts about something; human existence, finally, is rooted in time and tied to "the others." Man's *Sein* is a *Mit-sein,* as Heidegger, a philosopher who understood poets and knew that they make worlds with words, amply demonstrated. [6] Hence the poet's Angel remains in his eternity, a pure *essence* of unceasing knowledge that cannot comprehend [grasp] (t)his human *existence* — one marked by *Sorge* (sorga) Sorrow and *Angst/* anxiety — reflected in the image of the fountain.

---

[6] Martin Heidegger, *Sein und Zeit* (Tübingen: Max Niemeyer Verlag, 1977), esp. pp. 180 ff., "Die Sorge als Sein des Daseins," and pp. 231 ff., first section of "Dasein und Zeitlichkeit."

Yet man created gods, and Valéry, we recall, constructed his Angel's essence out of and against the very vulnerability of his human existence. "L'angoisse," reads an entry from the "Cahier B 1910" of *Tel quel,* "Angoisse, mon véritable métier. Et à la moindre lueur, je rebâtis la hauteur d'où je tomberai ensuite" (*O,* II, 588). And a *Notebook* entry from the twenties comments too on the Fallen Angel: "*Voici cinquante ans que je* TOMBE" (*Cahiers,* VIII, 373) [Valéry's emphases].

CHAPTER IX

MYTH AND METHOD

In tracing the Angel image in Valéry's *œuvre,* we observed that image, inherited from Romanticism and transformed by Symbolism, evolve in the young poet — and antipoet — to assume gradually the proportions of a personal myth, the hero of "toute une mythologie." Significantly, Valéry's Angel always remained a symbolic *image,* never slipping either into a pure *symbol* or simple intellectual concept; his maker remained, after all, a poet who never succeeded in the mathematics that inspired him — most fortunate failure! Valéry himself repeatedly insisted, moreover, on the Angel's *mytho*-logical dimensions, as in "Traités singuliers": "Je voyais toute une *mythologie de l'esprit....*" This notation also linked the Angel to various figures of his poetic universe, like Faust, Teste, Leonardo, and Sémiramis. And after the early Symbolist poems celebrating the Angel, we found that Angel's pervasive presence in fact hidden under a variety of masks or personae that fragmented the figure into its multifarious reflections. This fragmentation is the essence of a creative method that not merely informs but forms the myth.

In our earlier study of Valéry's prose *aubades,* we considered at length the emergence of the "mobile fragment," so characteristic of the poet's creative technique, and in that context intimately linked to the ever-repeated celebration of the privileged moment of renewal of the *Moi pur.* Our examination of the Angel, its major mythopoetic image, has revealed a similar fragmentation, again the result of Valéry's method of composition; it also suggests, moreover, the logic of his maker's predilection for that method, a method most clearly explained by Valéry himself in a *Notebook* passage of 1917 (*Cahiers,* VI, 473):

> Mon travail d'écrivain consiste uniquement à mettre en œuvre (à la lettre) des notes, des fragments écrits à propos de tout, et à *toute époque de mon histoire.* Pour moi traiter un sujet, c'est amener des morceaux *existants* à se grouper dans le sujet choisi bien plus tard par des circonstances, qui viennent comme ils veulent, quand ils veulent et sont ce qu'ils sont.

More than twenty years later, the poet notes in retrospect: "Mais je n'ai jamais réalisé mon système que par très petits fragments" (*Cahiers,* XXIV, 117); and he confirms: "Or cette œuvre toute mienne se réduit à des poèmes, à des fragments—et puis—mais surtout,—à mes idées plus ou moins notées..." (*Cahiers,* XXVI, 500). In tracing the Angel in the *œuvre,* we have thus been led by the poet himself to read not merely the poems, or "finished" texts, but the *Notebooks* which contain the essence of his thought, on the Angel as on any other subject which concerned him.

Our entire study, then, has been determined, ellipse-like, by two centers, the one a fundamental Valéryan myth of the Angel, the other a fundamental Valéryan creative method, the construct of fragments. Together, myth and method lead us very close to the heart of Valéry's creative process, and to the essential nature of the poet's mind. Even his earliest angels — those embedded within his youthful letters to Gide, those Symbolist angels whose maker had just "read great pages in Schopenhauer"[1] — are already fragments, separable parts of another form. And in them the myth itself had already begun to fragment into one of its numerous variants, in this case the angelic/anti-angelic vision of sad human introspection, "Narcisse, qui s'épleure en les bois bleus..."[2] Not coincidentally, even this early version of "Narcisse parle" (*O,* I, 1551-52) was labeled in its published form: "Fragment." Angel and Narcissus are fragmentary reflections of a fragmented self, the product of a "dédoublement intérieur," which early in life served to protect an immensely vulnerable Self that lay behind these poetic objectifications.

---

[1] *Gide-Valéry Correspondance,* p. 44.
[2] Ibid., p. 54.

For Valéry as *Ego scriptor*, in the beginning was the "regard d'Ange," productive of "mes idées plus ou moins notées," a *regard* at once lucid, impassive, seeing and circumscribing all with godlike — angelic — objectivity and remoteness while itself remaining unseen, uncircumscribed, observing with a sort of magnificent indifference the struggles of the vulnerable *Moi,* and thereby protecting the innermost ego from the consequences of those troubles. Thus it had protected him during childhood punishments, and thus it helped him recover from his earliest love. Thus also it remained significant to his poetry throughout his life. But this aloof Angel of the incurable Cartesian suffered its own defeats during the poet's mature life, most obviously during his deeply significant encounter with "Béatrice." In 1938 the older poet, looking back on the Self of 1892 ("La Révélation anagogique"), images it further fragmented into the "two terrible angels Nous and Eros" that together make up the "Antégo" against which the *Moi* fights, and with which it fuses, recognizing them as parts of itself. Thus, while Eros struggles with Nous, Body with Mind, Dionysian with Apollonian, Phi with Psi, the *Moi pur* somehow extricates itself and struggles like Jacob with the "Antégo" which emerges against it. The *Moi pur* who observes this struggle of Nous and Eros is yet a further psychic fragmentation, which recalls the infinitely regressing self-image suggested by Teste and the Young Fate, both of whom are observers of themselves observing. The efforts of the *Moi pur,* whatever its vehicle or persona, to escape existential limitations are unending in Valéry's *œuvre,* and hence the defeat of the inward Angel is foreordained. But here once again the delineation of a fragmented persona is itself a fragment; the last section of "La Révélation anagogique," and thus the entire structure, remains open-ended, unfinished and unpublished by its author, though one of his most significant "Broken Stories."

This text, moreover, provides an excellent example of another type of fragmentation common in Valéry. It designates its reader: "J'ai voulu 'écrire' pour moi, et en moi, pour me servir de cette connaissance, les conditions de limite ou fermeture...". In the *Notebooks,* Narcissus' reflection is, first of all, for himself; its reader is the *Ego scriptor* who projects his image in *his* text. "Pour me servir" points to the poet's method: he used those *Notebooks* all his life, to draw from them what circumstances called for, more often than not "sur commande." Valéry's implied reader, then, is fragmented as is the œuvre, into Self and Other, into various selves and into various others.[3] Valéry's title to the "*Anagogical* Revelation" obviously suggests the old fourfold method of interpretation, that is of reading a text. Is he not, perhaps ironically, alluding to its fragmentation? For no one was more aware of the reader's function in the literary process than this poet and writer of the *Notebooks*: "Si je prends des fragments dans ces cahiers et...que je les publie, l'ensemble fera quelque chose. Le Lecteur — et même moi-même—en formera une *unité*" (*Cahiers*, XVII, 892). Valéry is here foreseeing and referring to the reader's active role in what Roman Ingarden has called the "concretization" or "actualization" of the text(s).[4] And Valéry's ideal reader was, of course, modeled after himself, "ce lecteur idéal qui *existe* dans tout être qui écrit" (*Cahiers*, XXVII, 683).[5]

Valéry was aware, then, of the importance of his reader, and this awareness entered into his method of composition. For he relied on the reader to recognize the wholeness of the "author-structure" and that of the œuvre as a dynamic system, rather than the sum of its

---

[3] For a discussion of Valéry's reader, v. my "Valéry's Reader: 'L'Amateur de poèmes' ", in *The Centennial Review*, 22, 4, 389-99.

[4] Roman Ingarden, *The Cognition of the Literary Work of Art* (Evanston: Northwestern University Press, 1973), esp. pp. 94-145, "Temporal Perspective in the Concretization of the Literary Work of Art."

[5] Valéry, who also insisted that every poet is himself a critic, seems to have anticipated an orientation of modern criticism, usually labeled "Rezeptionsästhetik," and more recently represented by such scholars as Roman Ingarden, Wolfgang Iser, and the school of Hans Robert Jauss. In *Tel quel*, Valéry remarks: "Le critique ne doit pas être un lecteur, mais le témoin d'un lecteur, celui qui le regarde lire... L'opération critique capitale est la détermination du lecteur. La critique regarde trop vers l'auteur" (*O*, II, 557). Thus we disagree with Tzvetan Todorov when, in his discussion of "La 'poétique' de Valéry" (in *Cahiers Paul Valéry I: Poétique et poésie*, pp. 125-32), he concludes: "... deux théories complémentaires devront prendre en charge les relations entre œuvre et auteur ou lecteur. C'est à la première d'entre elles que correspond la 'poétique' de Valéry; la seconde semble devenir, de nos jours, l'objet d'études prometteuses (en Allemagne)" (pp. 131-32). Todorov bases his opinion solely on Valéry's "De l'enseignement de la poétique au Collège de France," "Leçon inaugurale du Cours de poétique du Collège de France," and "Cours de poétique," leaving out of account the *Cahiers*, or such excerpts from the *Notebooks* as those published in *Tel quel*.

fragments. He knew that the structural organization of his work and
its dominant themes — for example, that of the Angel — was not
"given" as such in his textual fragments, but would grow out of the
concretization of their virtualities. [6]

Thus with Teste, one of Valéry's most famous angelic heroes,
whom we encountered, again, in "un écrit, comme tous les miens,
de circonstance. Avec des notes vite assemblées, j'ai fait ce faux
portrait de personne." And here myth and method are so intimately
linked that the question of their reciprocal cause and effect — which
influenced which? — would lead us in a hermeneutic circle. Valéry's
alter-angeli — those personae into which the angel-image fragmented
repeatedly throughout the poet's life — are themselves all fragments:
fragmentary insights and reflections on the angel-fragments of the
whole man, sketched out in textual fragments scattered like the
Sibyl's leaves throughout Valéry's long creative life. Teste, as his
maker tells us, "est un personnage obtenu par le fractionnement
d'un être réel dont on extrairait les moments les plus intellectuels
pour en composer le tout de la vie d'un personnage imaginaire,"
and we found this fragmentary nature of the protagonist reflected
in the very form of this "roman moderne," namely the fragments
— letters, "extraits du log-book," dialogues, sketches and "pensées" — that together compose the "Cycle Teste." Nowhere is Valéry
more Cartesian than in this strange persona of the detached intellect.
And "Agathe" is one of *Teste*'s fragmentary reflections, a persona
for Teste's White Night.

Valéry's figure of Leonardo da Vinci is likewise an excellent
demonstration of the poet's creative method: the gradual refinement
of thought and expression by superimposing or laminating successive
fragments from widely different times of his life to produce, not
a final expression, but one which grows ever more mature. [7]

We noted that composition by fragments characterizes Valéry's
verse as well as his prose. Typical is his "Profusion du soir" which
the poet began in 1899, worked over periodically for more than
twenty years and at length published, unfinished, with the sub-title

---

[6] Cf. Felix V. Vodička, "Konkretisation des literarischen Werks" in *Rezeptionsästhetik* (München: Wilhelm Fink Verlag, 1975), esp. pp. 101 ff., "Die
Wandlung der Struktur des 'Autors' in der aktuellen Bewertung."
[7] We traced the history of the Leonardo texts in pp. 49-53.

"Poème abandonné." And we recall how Valéry himself had remarked that he was compelled to compose "La Jeune Parque" by fragments: "Je n'ai pu me tirer de l'affaire qu'en travaillant par morceaux." The poem's genesis has been examined by Florence de Lussy.[8] The entire volume of *Charmes* is enclosed as it were by two fragments, once part of the same poem: "Aurore" and "Palme," which remain related in form and vocabulary, but especially in their profound expression of those male and female sides of the human psyche, animus and anima. And the female aspect of the psyche — its maternity — is announced by one of Valéry's most lovely angels, his Angel of the Annunciation, Angel of Light, animus announcing life to anima. That division is also reflected in "Le Cimetière marin," described by the poet as one of the most personal of his poems. To all these we may add the prose poem sequence "A B C," fragment of an *Alphabet* which once again reflects the *Moi*'s division into animus and anima, "ange fait de lumière" and "femme endormie."[9]

But any overview of Valéry's vision of the world constrains us to return once more to his almost obsessive image for the divided self: Narcissus, closely related to the Angel from the poet's earliest creative efforts, and spanning his entire productive life, to that final poem, in which Narcissus explicitly fuses with the Angel, two masks of the same person, two personae of the same *Moi*. In this vision of the *Moi*'s ultimate and irretrievable fragmentation, Valéry's life-long Cartesian dualism takes its final vengeance: the vision is tragic and inescapable. "Il y a un Narcisse qui s'aime et un autre qui se hait" (*Cahiers*, VIII, 414) Valéry had noted; the angel is in the first image, the human reflection in the fountain in the other. For "l'esprit ne se reconnaît pas dans l'homme—et moi dans mon miroir" (*Cahiers*, XVIII, 45). These notations date from the 1920s and 30s respectively, but read like a single, unified meditation.

This fragmentation of the *Moi* is the very raison d'être of the *Cahiers*. Written, preserved, and consulted over the period of half a century, they *are* Narcissus' mirror; that fountain is the fountainhead of the poetry: "Narcisse. Le problème—et la poésie—de

---

[8] Florence de Lussy, *La Genèse de 'La Jeune Parque' de Paul Valéry* (Paris: Minard, 1975).

[9] Cf. our "The A B C's of Literary Commerce: Valéry's *Alphabet*," in *Romance Notes*, 21, 1, 1-7.

l'*objet*—l'oscillation entre l'objet et le sujet—qui est le problème
du moi et de son *fonctionnement*—n'est-ce pas le mythe du Narcisse"
(*Cahiers,* XII, 795)? The complexity of Valéry's dialogue with his
Narcissus-Notebooks is reflected again in the "Fragments du Narcisse," fragments not "put together" until 1926. [10] Narcissus' reflections in the œuvre, then, are fragmented and multiple, and always
the Angel lurks behind these reflections; the epigraph opening the
"Cantate du Narcisse," taken from the "Fragments du Narcisse"
of *Charmes,* is really an apostrophe to the Angel:

> O semblable! et pourtant plus parfait que moi-même,
> Ephémère immortel si clair devant mex yeux.

Yet another conjunction of angelic figure and composition by
fragments appears in the poet's creation and treatments of Sémiramis.
Again, the figure preoccupied Valéry in various forms for almost
forty years, his last version of a poem begun in 1899 making its
appearance in 1938. His most finished treatment of the figure is
his "Sémiramis: mélodrame en trois actes et deux interludes,"
presented in May 1934, at the Paris Opera to the music of Honegger.
In this case a sort of finality was forced on Valéry by his collaboration with the composer. But the "mélodrame" form was itself very
loose and fragmentary, the entire first act consisting of descriptive
prose and stage directions, which are by their nature fragmentary
— visions to be fulfilled by others. Valéry clearly looked on it and
his other "mélodrame," *Amphion,* as experiments unconcluded; of
them he said: "Ce ne sont d'ailleurs là que des essais et des approxi-
mations..."; as he liked to say about all his poetry.

---

[10] The first piece, originating from the "Narcisse parle," grew out of successive additions and was first published in 1919, then again in 1921 in *La
Revue Universelle* as "Narcisse (Fragments)," and in the same year in *La Nouvelle Revue Française* as "Narcisse," the editor explaining that it is the repro-
duction of a "fragment d'un poème en préparation de Paul Valéry intitulé
Narcisse." The second numbered fragment, or rather parts of it, also appeared
separately, in *L'Hommage à Paul Valéry* of 1922, entitled "Narcisse (Fragment),"
while another section of the piece appeared under the same title in the *Anthologie des poètes du Divan* in 1923; the entire second section was then published
in 1924 under the title "Étude pour Narcisse" in *l'Anthologie de la Nouvelle
Poésie française.* The third section had appeared separately in 1922, entitled
"Fragments du Narcisse" in *La Nouvelle Revue Française.*

Before returning to Valéry's important *Faust* fragments, we may glance briefly at two further texts which marry the myth of the Angel to the method of the fragment in such a way as to force on our attention the insoluble metaphysical problem which lay behind them: the free verse "Paraboles," written to accompany twelve watercolors by Loulou Albert-Lasard and culminating in a hymn to the Angels, and the notes in the "Cahier *Gladiator* 1920-1925" for a projected "L'Ange et l'amour," never completed. The act of collaboration forced Valéry to give an uncharacteristic finality to "Paraboles," but he nevertheless later reassembled some of its fragments to produce a "Psaume devant la bête," thus celebrating out of a single literary font both Angel and Beast, the two beings which share that purity which man lacks. The notes for "L'Ange et l'amour," with their Latin observations on the angel's intellectual nature on the one hand and his very human traits — "tristesse de l'ange" — on the other, again leave man and angel wholly divided into two personae: "Ange fait de lumière" and "femme endormie." Their meeting in love — intellect and affect, male and female — takes place likewise in the "Faust" fragments, which also remain perforce unfinished. The Angel dossier's fragments merely intimate what might have become of them had their creator been able to harmonize the human and the angelic — or, rather, the animal (phi) and the angelic (psi) natures of man into a unified whole. Their fragmentary state is thus intimately linked to an inner and existential conflict which could not be resolved — not in life, and not in art.

Valéry also tells us in his preface, "Au Lecteur de bonne foi et de mauvaise volonté," how he wrote his *Faust* fragments. In fact, the poet so persistently involves his reader in the creative history and method of his texts that these meta-texts orienting the reader become part of the work, their voice being that of the *scriptor*-persona that we call "Valéry." He thus establishes a certain complicity with his reader before and for the reading of the "real" text; in the case of the *Faust* fragments he manifests, moreover, a certain "anxiety of influence": [11]

---

[11] Cf. Valéry's statements in regard to "L'Ame et la danse" about Mallarmé's treatment of the subject. It is clear, moreover, that the shadow of Goethe haunted Valéry. We recall not merely the "Discours en l'honneur de Goethe"

> L'acte du génie de les cueillir [Faust and Mephistopheles]
> à l'état fantoche dans la légende ou à la foire, et de les
> porter...au plus haut point d'existence poétique, semblerait
> devoir interdire à jamais à tout autre entrepreneur de fic-
> tions de les ressaisir par leurs noms et de les contraindre
> à se mouvoir et à se manifester dans de nouvelles combi-
> naisons d'événements et de paroles. (O, II, 277)

And then Valéry explains how the Faust fragments, "his Faust,"
came into being: "Or, un certain jour de 1940, je me suis surpris
me parlant à deux voix et me suis laissé aller à écrire ce qui venait."
Again the fragmentary composition — manner and product — are
stressed: he worked quickly, "sans plan, sans souci d'actions ni
de dimensions"; and his product was vague and fragmentary, a
Faust III "qui pourrait comprendre un nombre indéterminé d'ouvrages plus ou moins faits pour le théâtre: drames, comédies, tra-
gédies, féeries selon l'occasion: vers ou prose, selon l'humeur, produc-
tions parallèles, indépendantes, mais qui, je le savais, n'existeraient
jamais..." He awaits an "occasion," perhaps a "commande," to
develop these various and most varied poetic treatments of the
theme.

The *Faust* fragments remained in their "unfinished" state; and
Bastet's collection of the unpublished Faust pieces explains why
Valéry's *Faust* had to remain, like most of the texts reflecting the
broken Angel, unfinished and fragmentary. While the *Lust* fragments
suggest a development of the unwritten scene(s) of the abandoned
"L'Ange et l'amour," this attempt, too, failed; and as the conflict
remained unresolved, the text was abandoned.

We found another great and fragmentary angelic text contemporary with the *Faust* fragments, that tale, Biblical in tone and
imagery, of the Angel's visitation of the couple "Elihu" and "la

---

(O, I, 531-53), but *Notebook* entries like "Mon cahier perpétuel est mon
'Eckermann.' (Il n'est pas besoin d'être Goethe pour s'offrir un fidèle inter-
locuteur)" (*Cahiers*, XXIX, 416). This is from Valéry's last *Notebook* of 1945.
In the same *Notebook*: "Ego-avril 45 — Je suis frappé lisant Robert d'Har-
court — *Goethe et l'Art de vivre* — de trouver quantité de 'phobies' et manies
communes à Goethe et à moi — avec telles différences essentielles, bien entendu.
Mais le nombre et l'énergie des traits communs sont remarquables.... Je trouve
aussi, dans cette lecture, des aspects de Goethe qui se trouvent *dans mon Faust*
et que j'ignorais avant d'écrire. ce *Faust*" (*Cahiers*, XXIX, 721).

fille de Chanaan," of the twenty-fourth *Notebook* which is so rich in entries on "Faust III." Some of the sections of the text end in "etc.," thus pointing to an inchoate plan for their eventual elaboration. But, most noteworthy, Elihu's moving justification for the human Eros — Valéry's *apologia pro vita* and *human* happiness — fails to convince an Angel, who, made of Light, cannot even comprehend the human — "formed of clay and so far from the Light." Likewise, Valéry's last Angel cannot comprehend Narcissus' image reflected in the fountain, with an unintelligible increment of tears.

Surrounded, then, by the evidence of these Angel-fragments — this heap of broken images, to misapply a phrase of T. S. Eliot — what can we say in summation? Is not the poet here standing witness, both by his chosen myth and his chosen method, to the irretrievable fragmentation of the human individual, and indeed the human species, *animal mixtum?* The reader returns almost by compulsion to that tragic vision given final form only months before Valéry's death: Narcissus-Angel gazing down, uncomprehending, at Narcissus-Man, who weeps. A single, infinitely suggestive image here comprehends in their entire complexity the *Angst* of an individual and the metaphysical tragedy of an epoch. This profound twentieth-century Cartesian accepts (unlike Eliot) the fractured world into which he was born, with its broken images; but in some intense moments of his vision, an Adam barred from Eden, he would have it otherwise. The persona — *Ego scriptor* — stands apart and records, but participates in both the tears of *Narcisse-Homme* and the astonishment of *Narcisse-Ange.*

Myth and method merge early in the Valéryan vision. In the beginning, as we suggested, was the "regard d'Ange," that cool, remote survey of reality, the abstract simplicity of pure intellect, sealing off antiseptically the knowing mind of divided Man from the suffering of the flesh-bound remnant. We have attempted to explain throughout these pages, the complexity of Valéry's angel-images, but those images are always — even when clothed in Biblical exteriors — in their essence the angels of the imperturbable theologian-metaphysicians of the Middle Ages: each a species in itself, their reason not discursive like man's which operates by composing and dividing, but intuitive, drawing immediately on species connatural to them, their knowledge godlike, since it was infused into them by God Himself.

Hence Valéry's lucid "regard d'Ange" is a summation of the persona's "immortal longings," the lust after pure reason unencumbered, the infinite, impossible desire of the dualist whose Angel is imprisoned in the Flesh. We saw how, and how often, the poet came fully and magnificently to terms with the flesh, not merely as *Ego scriptor,* but even in some of his Angel-heroes. Leonardo and Faust, mixed creatures both, in the end supplant Teste, and even Teste/Agathe must voyage through the night preserved faithfully by *corps,* by Phi. But Valéry knew well that this recognition of the beauty and dignity of *corps* did not solve the dilemma of broken Man, or broken Angel. We observed that for the dualist this fragmentation was resolvable neither in life nor in art. Man's Fall was into the fragmentation of *corps* and *esprit;* or the Fall of the Angel was into the captivity of the flesh. Such a vision has a faintly acrid Manichaean air, and this Valéry knew well.

Hence a certain metaphysical irony hangs over Valéry's roster of angelic heroes. Saint Thomas' angels have perfect knowledge, undeceivable and without falsehood, for they obtained that knowledge not by abstracting intelligible species from material objects, but by an intelligible outpouring, *per intelligibilem effluxum,* directly from God, at the same time that they received, in creation, their intellectual nature. But the "regard d'Ange" of Valéry's fallen Angel/ Man must penetrate the obscurity of matter, a matter which engulfs, while it serves, both the angel-observer and the reality observed. Matter, in other words, is Man's medium in all things, and the angelic simplicity, the purity of separate substances, beyond his attainment. We noted earlier Valéry's remark that there is indeed a God, but that He must be sought within the individual man. Hence the irony, and the pathos. The angels of Saint Thomas had received their knowledge by an infallible outpouring from the transcendent, infinite, omnipotent and omniscient God of Judeo-Christian tradition; the Angels in Valéry's multifarious personae receive theirs only by a groping introspection through the murky Self. Narcissus views Narcissus, and does not comprehend: the unity of knowledge — of life — is shattered, and the great poet's vision of the world is constrained to flow forth in an inexhaustible cascade of the fragmentary.

POSTSCRIPT

There can be no Conclusion — merely a breaking off, of the life of the poet, who died two months after writing "L'Ange," and of our reading, that can never bring us to a conclusive end. In this study, we have merely gathered up some of the Angel's fragments dispersed throughout the œuvre, and have tried to learn from the examination of the shards what the entire figure might have been. But the fragments do not fit together into a whole. Though incomplete forms and portions of the world of nature can often reveal what has been and what will be, the angelic shards of Valéry's poetic universe are neither remains of a unified gestalt, nor signposts to an evolution toward unity. We have instead recognized the Angel's fragmentary reflections in almost every major Valéryan figure, and our reading itself is thus perforce fragmentary, focusing merely on the angelic side of Teste, Leonardo, Sémiramis, Valéry's Faust and his Devil; yet we found no single "definitive" Valéryan Angel. The Annunciatory Angel of "Palme" and the Angel of Elihu were poetic reminiscences of the Biblical messengers, rather than those angelic characteristics internalized in the *Moi pur*. Nowhere, not even in the last poetic culmination of over twenty years' reflections in drafts and Notebooks, did the fragments make up a whole; they add up to a broken figure, the Valéryan trinity of the three in one divided: Angel and Narcissus, "Antégo(s)" both within and against the Self. In this manner, the broken figure reflects the human psyche; for it is the unwritten text on Man that Valéry's reader concretizes, or reconstructs, in deconstructing the textual fragments on the Angel. And, as the great mythic heroes always do, the "unreal" Angel reveals our human reality.

Yet the myth of the Angel permeates all of the poet's expression, for the Angel stands at the heart of Valéry's "mythology of the mind." In the "Petite Lettre sur les mythes," Valéry writes: "*Mythe* est le nom de tout ce qui n'existe et ne subsiste qu'ayant la parole pour cause" (*O*, I, 963-64), but, he continues,

> que serions-nous donc sans le secours de ce qui n'existe pas? Peu de chose, ... Les mythes sont les âmes de nos actions et de nos amours. Nous ne pouvons agir qu'en nous mouvant vers un fantôme. Nous ne pouvons aimer que ce que nous créons. (*O*, I, 966-67)

The myth of the Angel orients texts written over a period of fifty years, for both the Self and for the Other, for various selves and for various others. What Valéry said in one of his earliest *Notebooks* about that writing, the weaving and the reading of these texts, reflects the Angel:

> Je sens toutes ces chose que j'écris ici—ces observations, ces rapprochements comme une tentative pour lire un texte et ce texte contient des foules de fragments clairs. L'ensemble est noir. (*Cahiers,* II, 479)

LIST OF WORKS CITED

1. BOOKS

Valéry, Paul. *Œuvres.* 2 vols. Paris: Gallimard, 1957 and 1960.
———. *Cahiers.* 29 vols. Paris: Centre National de la Recherche Scientifique, 1957-1961.
———. *Cahiers.* 2 vols. ed. Judith Robinson. Paris: Gallimard, 1973 and 1974.
———. *Agathe.* Copyright Agathe Rouart Valéry, Paris: 1956.
———. *Alphabet.* Paris: Blaizot, 1976.
———. "A B C" in *Commerce: Cahiers trimestriels,* V (Automne 1925), 7-14.
———. "Cahier *Gladiator* 1920-1925." Dossier Paul Valéry, Bibliothèque Nationale, Paris.
———. "Catalogue Pré-Teste." N.º 113. Dossier Paul Valéry, Bibliothèque Jacques Doucet, Paris.
Paul Valéry, Exposition du Centenaire. Paris: Bibliothèque Nationale, 1971.
Valéry, Paul. *Collected Works,* ed. Jackson Mathews. Vol. 2. *Poems in the Rough,* translated by Hilary Corke. Princeton: Princeton University Press, 1969.
Valéry, Paul. *Lettres à quelques-uns.* Paris: Gallimard, 1952.
André Gide-Paul Valéry Correspondance 1887-1942. Paris: Gallimard, 1957.
Paul Valéry-Gustave Fourment Correspondance 1887-1933. Paris: Gallimard, 1957.
Mallarmé, Stéphane. *Œuvres complètes.* Paris: Gallimard, 1945.
Aigrisse, Gilberte. *Psychanalyse de Paul Valéry.* Paris: Editions Universitaires, 1964.
Bloom, Harold. *The Anxiety of Influence.* London: Oxford University Press, 1973.
Celeyrette-Pietri, Nicole. *Valéry et le Moi des Cahiers à l'œuvre.* Paris: Klincksieck, 1979.
———. *"Agathe" ou "Le Manuscrit trouvé dans une cervelle" de Valéry.* Paris: Lettres modernes, 1981.
Crow, Christine M. *Paul Valéry: Consciousness of Nature.* Cambridge: Cambridge University Press, 1972.
Franklin, Ursula. *The Rhetoric of Valéry's Prose Aubades.* Toronto: University of Toronto Press, 1979.
Gaède, Edouard. *Nietzsche et Valéry.* Paris: Gallimard, 1962.
Ingarden, Roman. *The Cognition of the Literary Work of Art.* Evanston: Northwestern University Press, 1973.
Johnson, Barbara. *Défigurations du langage poétique.* Paris: Flammarion, 1979.

Kunze, Peter. "Le Mythe de l'Ange dans l'œuvre de Paul Valéry." Diss. (thèse de troisième cycle, présentée à l'Université de Clermont II, U.E.R. Lettres, soutenue le 20 mars 1978).

Lawler, James R. *Lecture de Valéry*. Paris: Presses Universitaires de France, 1963.

──────. *The Poet as Analyst*. Berkeley: University of California Press, 1974.

Laurenti, Huguette. *Paul Valéry et le théâtre*. Paris: Gallimard, 1973.

Laurette, Pierre. *Le Thème de l'arbre chez Valéry*. Paris: Klincksieck, 1967.

Lazaridès, Alexandre. *Valéry pour une Poétique du Dialogue*. Montréal: Les Presses de l'Université de Montréal, 1978.

Levaillant, Jean. *La Jeune Parque et poèmes en prose*. Paris: Gallimard, 1974.

Livni, Abraham. *La Recherche du Dieu chez Paul Valéry*. Montréal: Presses de l'Université de Montréal, 1978.

Lussy, Florence de. *La Genèse de 'La Jeune Parque' de Paul Valéry*. Paris: Minard, 1975.

Mondor, Henri. *L'Heureuse Rencontre de Valéry et de Mallarmé*. Lausanne: La Guilde du Livre, 1947.

Nadal, Octave. *A Mesure haute*. Paris: Mercure de France, 1964.

Raymond, Marcel. *Paul Valéry et la tentation de l'esprit*. Neuchatel: A la Baconnière, 1948.

Riffaterre, Michael. *Semiotics of Poetry*. Bloomington: University of Indiana Press, 1978.

Robinson, Judith. *Analyse de l'esprit dans les Cahiers de Valéry*. Paris: Corti, 1963.

Rochefoucauld, Edmée de la. *En Lisant les Cahiers de Paul Valéry*. 3 vols. Paris: Editions Universitaires, 1967.

St. Hélier, Monique. *A Rilke pour Noël*. Bern: Editions du Chandelier, 1927.

Weinberg, Kurt. *The Figure of Faust in Valéry and Goethe*. Princeton: Princeton University Press, 1976.

Whiting, Charles C. *Valéry jeune poète*. Paris: Presses Universitaires de France, 1960.

Heidegger, Martin. *Sein und Zeit*. Tübingen: Max Niemeyer Verlag, 1977.

Nietzsche, Friedrich. *Werke in Zwei Bänden*. München: Carl Hanser Verlag, 1976.

Princeton Encyclopedia of Poetry and Poetics. Princeton: Princeton University Press, 1974.

2. ARTICLES

Austin, Lloyd J. "Paul Valéry compose *Le Cimetière marin*," *Mercure de France* (janvier-avril 1953), 600.

Barbier, Carl C. "Valéry et Mallarmé jusqu'en 1898," *Colloque Paul Valéry*. Paris: Nizet, 1978, 49-83.

Bastet, Ned. "L'Expérience de la Borne et du dépassement chez Valéry," *Cahiers Paul Valéry I: Poétique et poésie*. Paris: Gallimard, 1975, 57-90.

──────. "Faust et le cycle," *Entretiens sur Paul Valéry*. La Haye: Mouton, 1968, 115-28.

──────. "Textes inédits Quatrième acte de 'Lust,'" *Cahiers Paul Valéry II: "Mes théâtres"*. Paris: Gallimard, 1977, 51-158.

Franklin, Ursula. "'Les Vieilles Ruelles,' 'Pages inédites,' and 'Purs drames': A Dialectical Triad of Three Early Prose Poems by Paul Valéry," *Kentucky Romance Quarterly* (Summer 1979), 81-94.

Franklin, Ursula. "The A B C's of Literary Commerce: Valéry's *Alphabet*," *Romance Notes*, 22 (1981), 1-7.

———. "The White Night of *Agathe*: A Fragment by Paul Valéry," *Essays in French Literature*, 12 (November 1975), 37-58.

———. "Valéry's Reader: 'L'Amateur de poèmes,' *The Centennial Review*, 22 (1978), 389-99.

———. "A Valéryan Trilogy: The Prose Poems 'A B C'," *The Centennial Review*, 20 (1976), 244-56.

———. "Segregation and Disintegration of an Image: Mallarmé's Struggle with the Angel" (to appear in *Nineteenth-Century French Studies*).

———. "Structural Variations on a Theme: The Mobile Fragments of Valéry's Prose Aubades," *Michigan Academician*, 10 (1977), 163-79.

———. "Toward the Prose Fragment in Mallarmé and Valéry: *Igitur* and *Agathe*," *French Review*, 49 (1976), 536-48.

———. "The Angel in Valéry and Rilke," *Comparative Literature*, 35 (1983), 119-50.

———. "Mallarmé's Living Metaphor: Valéry's Athikté and Rilke's 'Spanish Dancer,'" *Pre-Text, Text, Context: Essays in Nineteenth-Century French Literature*. Columbus: Ohio State University Press, 1980, 217-27.

Lawler, James R. "Valéry et Mallarmé: Le Tigre et la Gazelle," *Colloque Paul Valéry*. Paris: Nizet, 1978, 85-103.

Sollers, Philippe. "Le représentant d'une culture finissante..." *Le Monde*, 29 août 1971.

Todorov, Tzvetan. "La 'poétique' de Valéry," *Cahiers Paul Valéry I: Poétique et poésie*. Paris: Gallimard, 1975, 125-32.

Toesca, Maurice. "Paul Valéry: Agathe," *La Nouvelle Revue Française*, n. s. 9 (mai 1957), 910-12.

Vodička, Felix, V. "Konkretisation des literarischen Werkes," *Rezeptionsästhetik*. Ed. Rainer Warning. München: Wilhelm Fink Verlag, 1975, 84-112.

NORTH CAROLINA STUDIES IN THE ROMANCE LANGUAGES AND LITERATURES

I.S.B.N. Prefix 0-8078-

Recent Titles

DELIE. CONCORDANCE, by Jerry Nash. 1976. 2 Volumes. (No. 174).

FIGURES OF REPETITION IN THE OLD PROVENÇAL LYRIC: A STUDY IN THE STYLE OF THE TROUBADOURS, by Nathaniel B. Smith. 1976. (No. 176). *-9176-2*.

A CRITICAL EDITION OF LE REGIME TRESUTILE ET TRESPROUFITABLE POUR CONSERVER ET GARDER LA SANTE DU CORPS HUMAIN, by Patricia Willett Cummins. 1977. (No. 177).

THE DRAMA OF SELF IN GUILLAUME APOLLINAIRE'S "ALCOOLS", by Richard Howard Stamelman. 1976. (No. 178). *-9178-9*.

A CRITICAL EDITION OF "LA PASSION NOSTRE SEIGNEUR" FROM MANUSCRIPT 1131 FROM THE BIBLIOTHEQUE SAINTE-GENEVIEVE, PARIS, by Edward J. Gallagher. 1976. (No. 179). *-9179-7*.

A QUANTITATIVE AND COMPARATIVE STUDY OF THE VOCALISM OF THE LATIN INSCRIPTIONS OF NORTH AFRICA, BRITAIN, DALMATIA, AND THE BALKANS, by Stephen William Omeltchenko. 1977. (No. 180). *-9180-0*.

OCTAVIEN DE SAINT-GELAIS "LE SEJOUR D'HONNEUR", edited by Joseph A. James. 1977. (No. 181). *-9181-9*.

A STUDY OF NOMINAL INFLECTION IN LATIN INSCRIPTIONS, by Paul A. Gaeng. 1977. (No. 182). *-9182-7*.

THE LIFE AND WORKS OF LUIS CARLOS LÓPEZ, by Martha S. Bazik. 1977. (No. 183). *-9183-5*.

"THE CORT D'AMOR". A THIRTEENTH-CENTURY ALLEGORICAL ART OF LOVE, by Lowanne E. Jones. 1977. (No. 185). *-9185-1*.

PHYTONYMIC DERIVATIONAL SYSTEMS IN THE ROMANCE LANGUAGES: STUDIES IN THEIR ORIGIN AND DEVELOPMENT, by Walter E. Geiger. 1978. (No. 187). *-9187-8*.

LANGUAGE IN GIOVANNI VERGA'S EARLY NOVELS, by Nicholas Patruno. 1977. (No. 188). *-9188-6*.

BLAS DE OTERO EN SU POESÍA, by Moraima de Semprún Donahue. 1977. (No. 189). *-9189-4*.

LA ANATOMÍA DE "EL DIABLO COJUELO": DESLINDES DEL GÉNERO ANATOMÍSTICO, por C. George Peale. 1977. (No. 191). *-9191-6*.

RICHARD SANS PEUR, EDITED FROM "LE ROMANT DE RICHART" AND FROM GILLES CORROZET'S "RICHART SANS PAOUR", by Denis Joseph Conlon. 1977. (No. 192). *-9192-4*.

MARCEL PROUST'S GRASSET PROOFS. *Commentary and Variants*, by Douglas Alden. 1978. (No. 193). *-9193-2*.

MONTAIGNE AND FEMINISM, by Cecile Insdorf. 1977. (No. 194). *-9194-0*.

SANTIAGO F. PUGLIA, AN EARLY PHILADELPHIA PROPAGANDIST FOR SPANISH AMERICAN INDEPENDENCE, by Merle S. Simmons. 1977. (No. 195). *-9195-9*.

BAROQUE FICTION-MAKING. A STUDY OF GOMBERVILLE'S "POLEXANDRE", by Edward Baron Turk. 1978. (No. 196). *-9196-7*.

THE TRAGIC FALL: DON ÁLVARO DE LUNA AND OTHER FAVORITES IN SPANISH GOLDEN AGE DRAMA, by Raymond R. MacCurdy. 1978. (No. 197). *-9197-5*.

A BAHIAN HERITAGE. An Ethnolinguistic Study of African Influences on Bahian Portuguese, by William W. Megenney. 1978. (No. 198). *-9198-3*.

"LA QUERELLE DE LA ROSE: Letters and Documents", by Joseph L. Baird and John R. Kane. 1978. (No. 199). *-9199-1*.

TWO AGAINST TIME. *A Study of the Very Present Worlds of Paul Claudel and Charles Péguy*, by Joy Nachod Humes. 1978. (No. 200). *-9200-9*.

When ordering please cite the *ISBN Prefix* plus the last four digits for each title.

Send orders to: University of North Carolina Press
 Chapel Hill
 North Carolina 27514
 U. S. A.

NORTH CAROLINA STUDIES IN THE ROMANCE LANGUAGES AND LITERATURES

I.S.B.N. Prefix 0-8078-

Recent Titles

TECHNIQUES OF IRONY IN ANATOLE FRANCE. Essay on *Les Sept Femmes de la Barbe-Bleue*, by Diane Wolfe Levy. 1978. (No. 201). *-9201-7.*

THE PERIPHRASTIC FUTURES FORMED BY THE ROMANCE REFLEXES OF "VADO (AD)" "PLUS INFINITIVE, by James Joseph Champion. 1978 (No. 202). *-9202-5.*

THE EVOLUTION OF THE LATIN /b/-/ʉ/ MERGER: A Quantitative and Comparative Analysis of the *B-V* Alternation in Latin Inscriptions, by Joseph Louis Barbarino. 1978 (No. 203). *-9203-3.*

METAPHORIC NARRATION: THE STRUCTURE AND FUNCTION OF METAPHORS IN "A LA RECHERCHE DU TEMPS PERDU", by Inge Karalus Crosman. 1978 (No. 204). *-9204-1.*

LE VAIN SIECLE GUERPIR. A Literary Approach to Sainthood through Old French Hagiography of the Twelfth Century, by Phyllis Johnson and Brigitte Cazelles. 1979. (No. 205). *-9205-X.*

THE POETRY OF CHANGE: A STUDY OF THE SURREALIST WORKS OF BENJAMIN PÉRET, by Julia Field Costich. 1979. (No. 206). *-9206-8.*

NARRATIVE PERSPECTIVE IN THE POST-CIVIL WAR NOVELS OF FRANCISCO AYALA "MUERTES DE PERRO" AND "EL FONDO DEL VASO", by Maryellen Bieder. 1979. (No. 207). *-9207-6.*

RABELAIS: HOMO LOGOS, by Alice Fiola Berry. 1979. (No. 208). *-9208-4.*

"DUEÑAS" AND "DONCELLAS": A STUDY OF THE "DOÑA RODRÍGUEZ" EPISODE IN "DON QUIJOTE", by Conchita Herdman Marianella. 1979. (No. 209). *-9209-2.*

PIERRE BOAISTUAU'S "HISTOIRES TRAGIQUES": A STUDY OF NARRATIVE FORM AND TRAGIC VISION, by Richard A. Carr. 1979. (No. 210). *-9210-6.*

REALITY AND EXPRESSION IN THE POETRY OF CARLOS PELLICER, by George Melnykovich. 1979. (No. 211). *-9211-4.*

MEDIEVAL MAN, HIS UNDERSTANDING OF HIMSELF, HIS SOCIETY, AND THE WORLD, by Urban T. Holmes, Jr. 1980. (No. 212). *-9212-2.*

MÉMOIRES SUR LA LIBRAIRIE ET SUR LA LIBERTÉ DE LA PRESSE, introduction and notes by Graham E. Rodmell. 1979. (No. 213). *-9213-0.*

THE FICTIONS OF THE SELF. THE EARLY WORKS OF MAURICE BARRES, by Gordon Shenton. 1979. (No. 214). *-9214-9.*

CECCO ANGIOLIERI. A STUDY, by Gifford P. Orwen. 1979. (No. 215). *-9215-7.*

THE INSTRUCTIONS OF SAINT LOUIS: A CRITICAL TEXT, by David O'Connell. 1979. (No. 216). *-9216-5.*

ARTFUL ELOQUENCE, JEAN LEMAIRE DE BELGES AND THE RHETORICAL TRADITION, by Michael F. O. Jenkins. 1980 (No. 217). *-9217-3.*

A CONCORDANCE TO MARIVAUX'S COMEDIES IN PROSE, edited by Donald C. Spinelli. 1979 (No. 218). 4 volumes, *-9218-1* (set); *-9219-X* (v. 1); *-9220-3* (v. 2); *-9221-1* (v. 3); *-9222-X* (v. 4.)

ABYSMAL GAMES IN THE NOVELS OF SAMUEL BECKETT, by Angela B. Moorjani. 1982 (No. 219). *-9223-8.*

GERMAIN NOUVEAU DIT HUMILIS: ÉTUDE BIOGRAPHIQUE, par Alexandre L. Amprimoz. 1983 (No. 220). *-9224-6.*

THE "VIE DE SAINT ALEXIS" IN THE TWELFTH AND THIRTEENTH CENTURIES: AN EDITION AND COMMENTARY, by Alison Goddard Elliott. 1983 (No. 221). *-9225-4.*

When ordering please cite the *ISBN Prefix* plus the last four digits for each title.

Send orders to: University of North Carolina Press
Chapel Hill
North Carolina 27514
U. S. A.

3 9001 01863 5071